D0176396

Lust for Enlightenment

Tachikawa-Ryū sex mandala. The two polar forces of the universe, manifested as male and female human beings, are joined in cosmic embrace within a lotus-shaped *yoni*. The character emanating from the center of the united couple is the mystic seed-syllable *A*, representing the origin of existence. The Tachikawa Ryū, a Japanese esoteric Buddhist sect, taught that sexual intercourse, if properly understood and practiced, was the surest way to supreme enlightenment.

Lust for Enlightenment

Buddhism and Sex

John Stevens

SHAMBHALA
Boston & London
1990

Shambhala Publications, Inc.
Horticultural Hall
300 Massachusetts Avenue
Boston, Massachusetts 02115

© 1990 by John Stevens
All rights reserved. No part of this book may be reproduced in any
form or by any means, electronic or mechanical, including pho-
tocopying, recording, or by any information storage and retrieval
system, without permission in writing from the publisher.

9 8 7 6 5 4 3 2 1

First Edition
Printed in the United States of America on acid-free paper
Distributed in the United States by Random House
and in Canada by Random House of Canada Ltd.

The author thanks the Dawn Horse Press for permission to quote
from *The Divine Madman*, © 1980 by Keith Dowman; Penguin
Books Ltd. for permission to quote from *Sky Dancer: The Secret Life
and Songs of the Lady Yeshe Tsogyel*, © 1984 by Keith Dowman; and
the State University of New York Press for permission to quote
from *Masters of Mahāmudra*, © 1985 by Keith Dowman.

Library of Congress Cataloging-in-Publication Data

Stevens, John, 1947–
    Lust for enlightenment: Buddhism and sex / John Stevens.—1st
ed.
        p.   cm.
    Includes bibliographical references (p.
    ISBN 0-87773-416-X (alk. paper)
    1. Sex—Religious aspects—Buddhism.   2. Religious life—
Buddhism.
    3. Buddhism—Doctrines.   I. Title
BQ4570.S48S74 1990   90-55065
294.3'422—dc20   CIP

If one's thoughts toward the Dharma
Were of the same intensity as those toward love,
One would become a Buddha,
In this very body, in this very life.

—THE SIXTH DALAI LAMA

Contents

Illustrations

PLATES FOLLOWING PAGE 92

Birth of the Buddha. Girandon/Art Resource.

Gotama with his harem. Courtesy of Roli Books International.

Sexual exhaustions. Nāgārjunakoṇḍa Archaeological Museum. Courtesy of UNESCO.

Gotama on an outing. Archaeological Survey of India.

Gotama bids farewell to his wife and son. Courtesy of the British Museum.

The fasting Buddha. Lahore Museum, Pakistan.

The last temptation of the Buddha. Courtesy of UNESCO.

A puritan Buddhist elder. Courtesy of the British Museum.

Lord and Lady of Secrets. Collection of John Stevens.

Heavenly maiden, from a Buddhist temple in Sri Lanka. Courtesy of John Calman & King.

Lush Buddhist beauty, from a Buddhist shrine in Mathura, India. Courtesy of John Calman & King.

Kannon, Buddhist goddess of compassion. The Gitter Collection.

Zen and the reality of sex. (a) Calligraphy by Ikkyū, Okayama Art Museum, Japan; (b) calligraphy by Zuiun, private collection.

Phallic symbol by Hakuin. Genshin Collection.

Double portrait of Ikkyū and his blind lover Lady Mori. Masaki Art Museum, Japan.

The Bath. Shōka Collection.

Daruma captivated by a courtesan by Kawanabe Kyosai. Private collection.

Zen "breast" garden, Daitoku-ji, Kyoto.

Buddhist monks and a nun misbehaving themselves. Two Japanese woodblock prints, courtesy of the Gichner Foundation.

Preface

Enlightenment has a physical dimension as well as a spiritual one. Over the centuries, Buddhists have responded to the urgent reality of sex, the basic fact of existence, in a variety of fascinating (and frequently contradictory) ways, reflecting the multifaceted manner in which human beings relate to the inner fire that sparks all life. Throughout history, for example, puritan Buddhists who have attempted to ruthlessly suppress their sexuality in order to attain release have coexisted with Tantric Buddhists who wholeheartedly cultivated that same primal force, believing it to be an expedient to enlightenment. Buddhists, like everyone else, have always been perplexed by the sensitive subject of sex. Nevertheless, it is an element that lies at the core of our existence, and the nature of sex is a problem that must be grappled with by every religion and philosophy.

This is the first comprehensive survey of sexuality within the panorama of the "Buddhist experience." While it is true that Buddhism has a history that can be more or less described in objective terms, the message itself is hardly limited to historical events or documentary evidence. The Buddhist experience, mythological as well as historical, is all-encompassing. It includes meditation practice, oral transmission, instruction by example, written texts, sacred art and liturgy, ancient lore and traditions, personal encounters, universal intuitions, and transforming realizations. Those factors have remained essentially the same regardless of era and area.

Thus, on the highest levels, it is not correct to speak of the "development" of Buddhism. External conditions have changed, of course, and the mode in which Buddhism is expressed differs in each generation, but the inner elements of the Buddhist experience—the quest for enlightenment; the realization that life is impermanent, imperfect, and selfless; the overcoming of craving, hatred, and delusion; the transformation of body and mind; and the emphasis on deep insight and all-embracing compassion—are ever present. No matter what the time or place, Buddhists—and all human beings—have been confronted by the same existential questions that we face today. Paramount among these questions are "What is the true meaning of sex?" and "How should men and women relate to each other?"

Meeting the challenge of those questions head-on, I ask the reader to join me in a journey through the vast vistas of the Buddhist experience, created over thousands of years in countless lands among all manner of human beings, in order to plumb the depths and scale the heights of human sexuality.

1
The Sex Life of the Buddha

The Buddhist experience relies on higher truths, and it does not really matter, ultimately, whether or not there was a historical Buddha; however, the traditions and legends that surround the life and teaching of Gotama, the Awakened One, born in what is now Nepal sometime around 500 B.C.E., are based on perceptions that shape the Buddhist vision of the universe.

Even texts compiled by puritan Buddhists contain a wealth of information on his birth, early manhood, and sexual experiences, and it is not difficult to flesh out the romantic legend of Gotama in loving detail.[1]

The requisites for being the mother of a Buddha, for instance, are clearly delineated: she must be beautiful in facial appearance, figure, limb, and bearing; virtuous, of pleasant disposition, polite, patient, modest, chaste, obedient, reflective, and religious-minded; gracious and not facetious or quarrelsome; skilled at feminine pursuits; pure in body, mind, and speech; free of evil thoughts, anger, hatred, and the "faults of ordinary women."[2]

Queen Māyā met all these requirements and was a stunning beauty as well: dark, perfumed curls surrounded her unblemished, perfectly proportioned face; her eyes were clear as a blue lotus leaf and her lips red as a rose; her teeth shone as brightly as the stars in the sky, her breath was as fragrant as incense, and her voice as soft as a dove's; her body was smooth, firm, and lusciously shaped. Queen Māyā was, in short, ravishing to the eye and heart, "radiant, alluring, and gleaming with a sheen of gold," so comely that even the gods envied her. In fact, she was called Māyādevi, "Goddess of Illusion," because her body was too beautiful to be believed.[3] Her husband, King Śuddhodana, was the ideal mate, supremely hand-

1

some, with a powerful, well-formed body, and neither too young nor too old.

Although the mother of a Buddha need not be a virgin, she must not have borne a child, and once the would-be Buddha enters her womb she naturally becomes devoid of all lustful thoughts and emotions.

That is why, it is said, when Queen Māyā realized she had conceived "spiritually"—tradition states that the Buddha-to-be descended into her womb as she slept—she asked her husband to allow her to take a vow of celibacy (along with vows not to kill, lie, steal, cheat, slander, engage in worldly talk, or be covetous, angry, or foolish). The king readily agreed and, we are told, thereafter regarded her as he would his mother or sister.

Exactly ten (lunar) months later, Māyā gave birth to a child unsullied by blood, mucus, or other discharge. The newborn was perfectly formed and was able to speak and walk, startling everyone present by immediately taking seven steps and declaring himself "the Honored One of Heaven and Earth." He received a natal bath from two water dragons, and flowers poured down from the sky. Seven days later Queen Māyā suddenly died,[4] and the infant was adopted by Mahāprajāpatī, his mother's sister and his father's second wife.

Not long after Gotama's birth, a soothsayer named Asita visited the palace to examine the unusual child. "This boy is destined to become a great leader," the sage declared solemnly. "If he remains in the palace he will become a universal monarch, but if he enters the religious life he will become an enlightened being, a teacher of men and gods."

The king, determined to make the first prediction of Asita come true, lavished care and attention on his son. He was raised by a host of doting wet nurses and nannies, and when he grew older nothing was denied him. Gotama used only the sweetest-smelling incense and wore the finest, most costly cloth; day and night a canopy shielded him from heat, cold, wind, and dust; he had three magnificent residences, one each for summer, winter, and the rainy season; the choicest delicacies graced his table; he was serenaded from morning to night by court musicians; and servants were always on hand to cater to his every need.

Gotama grew into an extraordinarily handsome prince with all the marks of a world conqueror: [5] he was well built and agile, with cool, smooth skin; he had golden hair (in some accounts), intense black (or dark blue) eyes, perfectly symmetrical features, a lustrous complexion, and a voice of the purest tones. His well-formed sex organs were "enclosed in a sheath," so that they were hidden from view even when he was naked. (That unusual characteristic explains why most statues of Gotama do not show even a hint of his private parts.) [6]

In order to further bind the prince to worldly life, the king decided to find him a chief consort and devised the following plan to secure the best bride for the finicky Gotama: "I'll have heaps of jewelry made for the prince to distribute as gifts to all the eligible maidens of the land and instruct my aides to carefully observe which of the girls catches the eye of my son." [7]

On the appointed day, however, the girls gathered at the palace merely swooned in the presence of the dashing prince, and Gotama did not appear to be interested in any of them. Suddenly, though, at the very end of the reception, a stunning beauty appeared with a huge entourage in tow. The lovely maiden walked up to the prince without hesitation, looked him directly in the eyes, and asked for her present.

"I am sorry," the prince said as he gazed back, "the jewelry is all gone. You should have come sooner."

"Why didn't you save something for me?" she asked in a hurt voice.

"Here, you can have my ring. Or how about my necklace?"

"No, thank you," said the girl petulantly, and she turned away as Gotama watched in rapt attention. (In another version, the girl took the necklace but added with a coy smile, "Is this all I am worth?") [8]

A full report of the encounter between Gotama and the girl, whose name was Yaśodharā (or Gopā in some accounts), was given to the king. When he was told how their eyes met and of Gotama's obvious fascination with the elegant maiden, the king immediately sent a messenger to Yaśodharā's father to ask for her hand on behalf of the prince. To his chagrin, the king was rebuffed: "I will consent to give my beloved daughter only to the young man who can prove he is superior to all the others."

3

An assembly of all the young men in the kingdom was quickly arranged, and Gotama squared off against the others in contests of writing, arithmetic, archery, swordsmanship, horse-riding, and boxing. Gotama emerged victorious in all the events and claimed his willing prize. They were married in a magnificent ceremony, and court poets sang that the fair Yaśodharā afforded the prince every sort of pleasure as they spent themselves in nuptial bliss—a delightful union of the choicest butter and the finest ghee.[9]

Yaśodharā was an independent sort, refusing to don a veil in the presence of her in-laws, the king and queen, and, more scandalously, in front of the other men of the household. When criticized for such behavior Yaśodharā replied, "A noble woman, one who guards the mind and controls the senses, will be properly veiled even if she happens to be naked—one cannot cover up sins with a pile of robes and a veil."[10]

As was the custom in those times, Gotama apparently had several other official wives[11]—one for each of his palaces?—and his courtship with the one known as Gotamī is also classic romance.[12]

The beauty Gotamī was desired by hundreds of suitors, but the girl, just as independent as Yaśodharā, steadfastly rejected all offers of an arranged match, even with the king's son, and insisted on making her own choice. "Let it be known that in one week I will select a husband. Have all the eligible men gather in the palace."

On the morning of the seventh day, Gotamī bathed in scented oil, decorated herself with the prettiest of flowers, put on her finest jewelry and robes, and made her way to the palace with her mother and several other attendants along to act as advisors. Surveying the crowd of dandies dressed to the teeth in fabulous garments and elaborate coiffures, weighted down with jewelry and reeking of perfume, Gotamī exclaimed with disgust, "These fops all look like women! They are more dressed up than I am!"

"Isn't there anyone here who catches your fancy?" her mother asked.

"Yes. One, and only one. That prince over there in the simple robe and radiant smile. At last, a real man."

In one text the girl is named Splendor of Delight, and she calls out to the prince:

4

When I saw you, young man, excellent
In form and strength, endowed with virtue,
All my senses were delighted,
And immense joy arose in me.

Your complexion is like a pure shining jewel,
Your hair is black and curly,
You have a fine brow and nose;
I offer myself to you.

You have excellent features.
Resplendent, you are like a mountain of gold.
In your presence I do not shine;
I am like a pile of charcoal.

Your eyes are large and dark,
Your jaw is like a lion's, your face like the full moon.
The fine sound of your voice is irresistible;
Please take me in.

Your tongue is long and broad,
Coppery red, soft, shining like a jewel;
With your superb, clear voice
You delight people when you speak.

Your teeth are even, shining white,
Clean and well-spaced;
When you show them as you smile,
You delight people, O hero.

Then the girl's mother, the supreme courtesan called Beautiful,
extols her daughter's charms to the prince:

With dark hair, lotus-blue eyes,
A clear voice, and golden complexion,
Finely clad in garlands, she emerged
From the lotus, resplendent as pure light.

Her limbs are bright, her body evenly balanced;
Her limbs are complete, her body well-proportioned;

5

> She shines like a golden statue adorned with jewels
> Illuminating all directions.
>
> The finest fragrance of sandalwood wafts from her body,
> Filling the air around her;
> As she speaks, with celestial sweetness,
> A scent like a blue lotus comes from her mouth.
>
> Whenever she smiles,
> Heavenly music plays;
> This treasure of a woman should not be abandoned
> To control of the vulgar.
>
> She is not short or too tall,
> Not stout or too thin;
> She is slender at the waist, full-breasted,
> Suitable for you with an impeccable body.[13]

A splendid ceremony was performed, and the couple retired to the palace to partake of the joys of wedded life.

Since the king's ministers suggested that the prince be enticed with all the pleasures of love in order to keep him addicted to the palace, in addition to his wives Gotama was waited on by an army of the most beautiful, accomplished, and adoring women in the kingdom, all vying to provide him the utmost in attention, service, amusement, and comfort.

It is possible to conjure up an idea of what these pleasure girls looked like from ancient Indian texts on love and classical Hindu and Buddhist iconography—indeed, Buddhist iconography is distinguished by its lavish use of the female form in all its sensuous glory.[14]

A pleasure girl of the Buddha's time was typically dressed in a red and gold girdle, with bracelets around her wrists and ankles. Her long, jet-black hair was adorned with flowers and ornaments. She possessed a face as lovely as the full moon, with doe eyes, a delicate nose, and red lips set off against a golden complexion. Naked above the waist, she wore necklaces and strings of pearls to grace her swelling, close-set breasts, which were shaped like golden cups, black-nippled, and rubbed with sandalwood oil. Her skin was as soft as rose petals; her navel was deep, her belly rounded with soft folds of skin, her hips ample, her buttocks high and firm, and her thighs like the stem of the banana tree. Her *yoni* (vulva) resembled a lotus bud and had the fragrance of a newly burst lily or fresh honey. She had a voice a cuckoo would envy, and she moved like a swan. The girl was well-versed in the arts of speaking, singing, dancing, and playing musical instruments; she was a teller of erotic tales, a weaver of spells, a creator of aphrodisiacs and potent perfumes.

Supremely skilled in the practice of love, having been taught by the sages of divine love, she was expert in imparting bliss to her partner; she was a sexual gymnast of the highest order. The girl was a master of the various types of kisses—moderate, contracted, pressed, soft, clasping, throbbing, the "war of tongues," the "secret of the upper lip"—and all other forms of oral love: side-biting, outside pressure, inside pressure, "kissing the stalk," "sucking a mango," "swallowing up." She was talented in every sort of embrace, familiar with the most effective love bites and scratches, and well-schooled in the techniques of physical union—widely open, yawning, clasping, twining, feet in the air, one leg up, inverted, reversed, supported, suspended, rising, all-encompassing, "packed," and the other specialties: "wheel of love," "opening and blossoming," "the bow," "splitting a bamboo," "fixing a nail," "pair of tongs," "spinning top," "the swing," and the postures of the crab, the tortoise, the crow, the monkey, the cow, the mare, the bird, the jumping tiger, the union of cats, the pressing of an elephant, the rutting of the boar, the bee buzzing over the honey, and (with another girl) the union of three. The girls also teamed up to perform the *yogini chakra* with the prince, a rite in which he made love simultaneously with three, five, seven, or nine partners.[15]

The king had a special "chamber of love" constructed for Gotama, decorated with erotic art and illumined with subdued light "like that of the hazy autumn sun."[16] Captivated by sexual extravagance, the prince spent his days and nights in continual dalliance, experiencing every imaginable sensual delight of heterosexual intercourse with the indefatigable beauties of his vast harem and, when he tired of them, with the professional goddesses of love in neighboring pleasure groves.[17] Gotama's life consisted largely of opening women's skirts, unfastening their girdles, pressing their swelling

7

An Indian prince sporting with members of his harem. This kind of elaborate dalliance was one of the prerogatives of an Indian prince such as Gotama. In fact, in his case it was probably even more extreme since Gotama's father, warned that his son might someday renounce the world and became a religious teacher, made certain that Gotama had constant access to every sort of heterosexual pleasure.

breasts, caressing their secret parts, and devouring them with love.[18] So intense was Gotama's lust that even the miracles attributed to him had to do with sex: Once in hot pursuit of one of his maidens, Gotama inadvertently stepped off the roof of the palace and found himself suspended in midair.[19]

Gotama's life revolved around the five elements of physical delight—beautiful women, excellent music, pleasing scents, fine food, and the best in raiment—corresponding to the senses of sight, hearing, smell, taste, and touch.

Yet despite his incomparable comfort, the prince was not at ease. His father made every effort to shield the prince from anything remotely unpleasant or upsetting by imprisoning him in a fantasy land, but Gotama was sorely troubled by his rare glimpses of the real world. Once, as a boy, he was taken to a plowing festival that marked the beginning of the planting season. Instead of enjoying the festivities, Gotama was appalled at the sight of sweat pouring off the men and oxen as they scarred the earth with their plows. Blood dripped from the bridles of the struggling oxen as man and beast strained and suffered in the scorching sun. Flocks of birds swooped down to feast on the hapless insects unearthed by the plow, and hawks, in turn, preyed upon the smaller sparrows and swallows. Filled with pity at the plight of all these creatures, the prince said to his father, "I need to be alone," and he went to sit beneath a tree to contemplate the meaning of it all.

Years later, Gotama received several more rude shocks. Despite the king's command to clear the streets of all refuse, material and human, when the prince was on an outing, Gotama was eventually confronted with the three ugliest facts of life. First he encountered a decrepit old man, bald, toothless, bent with age, racked by a rasping cough, staggering along on crutches; next he saw a diseased person with a swollen belly and crooked limbs, pale and miserable, covered with filth and flies and gasping for breath; then he witnessed a shroud-covered corpse being carried through the streets, the dead man's relatives following behind wailing terribly and beating their breasts. When he asked his attendant the significance of each incident he was told, "All human beings face the same fate."

After each of these frightful experiences Gotama tried to further abandon himself to the world of the senses, but to no avail—he became increasingly self-absorbed and withdrawn. On another trip outside, Gotama caught a glimpse of a serene mendicant monk; the homeless sage seemed to be at peace with himself and with the world. Gotama was neither, and he cut short his trip in disgust with himself and returned to the palace. On the way back, one of the young women who thronged to the balconies for a glimpse of the dashing prince as he drove by saw him and sang out his praises:

> Blessed indeed is the mother, blessed indeed is the father, blessed indeed is the wife of such a glorious Lord!

Upon hearing that, Gotama realized that he would only truly be blessed when he solved the riddle of life. In appreciation for the girl's prompting, Gotama sent her a pearl necklace (which she mistakenly took as a declaration of his love for her). Thereafter, he longed to break free from the confines of his pleasure palace and seek the truth before his mind was hopelessly clouded and his spirit totally debauched.

The king and Gotama's stepmother sensed the prince's growing dissatisfaction with his life; Mahāprajāpatī ordered the concubines to envelope the prince in "a cage of gold," taking care never to staunch the flow of narcotic wine or erotic entertainment.[20] In desperation, the king invited all the damsels in the realm to sport with the prince in a pleasure garden. The girls—intoxicated by wine, redolent of sweet perfume, and overcome with desire—rubbed against the prince with their fragrant breasts, and wrapped their legs around him. They slipped out of their robes and made every sort of tantalizing proposal, all to no avail.[21] Gotama's heart was elsewhere. "How can there be mirth and laughter," he sighed, "with so much suffering present in the world?"[22]

Gotama's closest friends were sent by the king to remind the prince of his duties toward the country and the women who lived only to love him. "How can you be unhappy with all this when you are so young and full of life? Follow tradition, and abandon the world when you are an old man."

Gotama's chief consort Yaśodharā had a nightmare about his leaving her and their newborn son. She was the only one who still had a hold on Gotama, and it is recorded that he consoled her gently and spent that night in loving embrace with her.[23]

Still, Gotama was in torment. When his anguished father asked, "What is the matter? Name your heart's desire and it will be yours," Gotama replied, "Promise me that I will always be youthful; that I will never be sick; and that I will never die. Promise that I will not lose you, nor the girls in my harem, nor my kinfolk. Promise me that this kingdom will never crumble or be plagued by evil." Those were wishes that even the greatest king could not grant. Palace life began to suffocate the prince.

Gotama's gloom spread over the kingdom. Birds stopped singing; flowers ceased to bloom; lakes and rivers dried up; crops withered; musical instruments shattered; and people became fitful.[24]

One night, following what was evidently a frenzied orgy, Gotama awoke from a troubled sleep and took a hard look at the harem women surrounding him in the love chamber. Lying about in torn clothing and disheveled hair, with their ornaments, tiaras, and musical instruments strewn about, the girls were far from a pretty sight. Some were naked, contorted into unseemly positions with legs and arms askew; others were snoring loudly with their mouths agape, mumbling to themselves in their sleep or drooling in a drunken stupor. In the lurid light of the oil lamps, the girls had lost all their allure—for the first time Gotama noticed the blemishes and flaws of each girl. Revolted by such meaningless excess, he felt as if he had come to in a cemetery full of the living dead.[25]

Gotama sighed wearily:

> This world is full of deception and falsehood
> and nothing is more deceiving than a woman's appearance;
> Attracted to fine clothes and trinkets,
> Foolish men become mad with desire,
> But when one realizes that a woman's charms are mere
>   illusion,
> He will no longer be deceived.
> This is the way to liberation and purity of body and mind.[26]

The repugnance Gotama now felt toward his life of frivolity and hedonism in the palace galvanized the prince, and he resolved to flee "this swampland of sex"[27] that very night to seek a path of deliverance.

Before fleeing the place, though, as legend maintains, Gotama had a last look around his domain and went to Yaśodharā's chambers to gaze upon his wife and son. The infant was sleeping peacefully next to his mother's breast, and Gotama moved to embrace him.

"No, I cannot," the prince whispered, restraining himself. "If I lift the queen's arm I will disturb her and waken them both. When I attain the truth I will be back to see them."[28]

So saying, Gotama summoned his faithful servant, the groom Chandaka, and called for his horse. Chandaka made a final appeal against Gotama's act. Among many other objections, Chandaka protested, "If you remain here and become, according to the prediction, a universal monarch, you could establish a kingdom of peace and plenty and create tremendous good."

11

But Gotama replied, "Even if I became ruler of the world and were able to provide my subjects with every physical need, they would still suffer from sickness, old age, and death. If I attain enlightenment, I can cure the spiritual anguish of all beings."

Gotama resolutely went forth from the palace into the gloom to seek enlightenment. The next morning he exchanged his silk robes for the tattered rags of a woodsman and shaved off his luxurious curls with his sword, symbolizing his renunciation of sex. (Long hair was believed to represent sexual vitality.) He then instructed Chandaka to return to the palace and report that Gotama was now a pilgrim who swore never again to be beguiled by sensual pleasure.

Upon his return, Chandaka found the palace in an uproar at the loss of the beloved prince. When told of Gotama's decision to flee, Yaśodharā beat her breast, tore at her clothes, ripped off her jewels and adornments, and made this heart-rending lament:

> He says he wants to practice the Dharma, but how can he do so by abandoning me, his faithful spouse? Is he ignorant of the ancient tradition of taking one's partner along in retirement from the world? He is not following the Dharma in regard to me, that is certain. Is there something the matter with me? Even if he finds what he is after, that is no reason to desert me and our new-born son, a child who will never be cradled on his father's lap. How hard-hearted and cruel he is—is there something wrong with my wish to be with him always? [29]

On and on she wept:

> Two human beings cherished each other:
> He was my joy, my sole delight.
> His face was as radiant as the moon
> And his form beyond compare.
> Without him, all my possessions are nothing
> but rubble.
> All alone on the bed we once shared,
> He has abandoned me . . .
> Henceforth I will not be able to take
> food and drink with pleasure;
> My hair will grow foul and matted;
> How tragic the forcible parting of two lovers! [30]

Chandaka consoled the queen by telling her of Gotama's determination to win enlightenment for the good of all, and of his promise to return when he found the answers he was seeking. The queen eventually recovered, at least in part, from her grief, and life went on.

Gotama's quest for enlightenment had begun.

His first stop was a grove where ascetics gathered to subjugate the flesh in order to release the soul from the shackles of the body. The ascetics were as dedicated to pain as the inhabitants of Gotama's former palace were devoted to pleasure. They survived, barely, on roots, wild vegetables, seeds, tree bark, cow dung, and the tiniest drops of water. If they dressed at all it was in rough animal skins, rags, hair shirts, or robes of weeds. They slept out in the open, in cemeteries, in caves, or in trees. The grim ascetics mortified themselves in a variety of ingenious ways: never bathing, standing continually submerged in water or mud, staring into the sun, sitting in the center of a ring of bonfires, locking themselves permanently into one posture or position and tearing their hair out by the roots or, on the other extreme, letting their hair grow until it was filthy and matted and then weighting it with chains.

Gotama was not convinced by the ascetics' argument that such severe penance would lead to inner peace: "If suffering is all there is to salvation, most of brute creation would have attained liberation aeons ago." When told by the ascetics that animal (and human) sacrifice produced great merit, Gotama replied, "Nonsense! Infliction of injury on other beings can never bring good fortune; all sacrifice is a vain attempt to bribe the gods." Gotama also rejected the ascetics' contention that the aim of the religious life is to gain a better rebirth. "Enlightenment in this very body is all that matters," he insisted.

After leaving the ascetics, Gotama called on the philosophers. He encountered amoral nihilists who maintained that all human morality and goodness were futile; materialists who claimed that existence was meaningless and ended totally at death; and yogins who advocated quiescent states of mind suspended between existence and non-existence, thought and non-thought. Gotama was not satisfied with either the materialists or the spiritualists; both, he sensed, offered distorted, partial views. Confused yet determined,

13

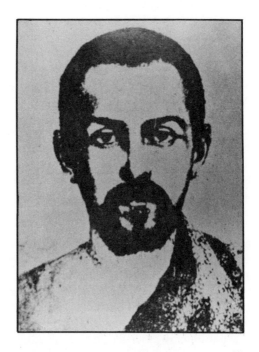

Buddha, the Enlightened One. This image, based on ancient Indian oral and visual tradition, is thought to best represent Buddha as he actually appeared. As a Buddha, Gotama was completely free of all sexual impulses; such impulses were extinguished upon his entry into nirvana.

Gotama traveled until he found an ideal spot for solitary meditation, a little hamlet near the lovely Nairañjanā River and the village of Uruvelā. Gotama said to himself, "The river here flows clear and clean, flowers, fruit, and green herbs are abundant, and the birds never stop singing. This quiet, peaceful place is perfect for my training."

There Gotama vowed to gain complete control of his body and mind by ridding himself of all passions, physical and mental. He sat in the meditation posture intently suppressing every thought, his effort so great that sweat poured from his body even in midwinter. To further calm his mind, Gotama stopped breathing for longer and longer periods, until his head was ready to explode. Further he went, attempting to starve his body into submission while horse-flies, mosquitoes, and other insects feasted on his flesh. Near the end of his six-year fast, Gotama was reduced to a skeleton, his limbs were blackened, knotty stems, his ribs stuck out like the beams of an old shed, and his spine could be grasped from the front. His head resembled a withered gourd, his eyes were as glazed as the water on the bottom of a nearly dry well, and his skin was the color of cremation ashes. No longer human in form, Gotama was taken for a dust demon by the village children, who cast garbage on him. Finally he collapsed and was left for dead.

Gotama slowly regained consciousness, dragged himself to the river, and washed away six years of grime and filth. A village girl gave him a nourishing bowl of *pāyāsa,* which restored and refreshed the exhausted seeker.

Pāyāsa, rice cooked with milk and mixed with crystal sugar and fragrant spices, is a special, costly delicacy. Gotama's acceptance of that dish, from a woman, indicated that he had come full circle. In the palace Gotama had partaken of the choicest delicacies; as a mendicant he had to suppress his disgust and eat whatever scraps were put into his bowl. He nearly fasted to death, but then ate rich food to regain his physical and mental vigor. Gotama had come to experience every type of sensation regarding food, ranging from gustatory delight to revulsion and from satiety to starvation. Also, he took the food from a lovely young woman without desiring or shying away from her beauty and sexual presence, for in that realm too he had experienced every possible variation regarding sex, from uninhibited indulgence[31] to absolute abstinence.

Now with his mind and body in proper balance, Gotama was ready to make a final attempt at release. He made a comfortable seat of thick grass beneath the cooling shade of a large tree, faced the east, placed himself in the meditation posture, and gazed out into the vastness of space. He resolved, "Even if my body dries up and

my skin, flesh, and bones wither away, I will not stir from this seat
until enlightenment is mine!"

First Gotama had to confront his inner demons of fear, loathing,
doubt, confusion, and malevolence, personified by the horrible
army of Māra, the Evil One. That dreadful horde consisted of
every imaginable type of awful monster and repulsive demon.
Gotama held firm, and the initial attack of the Devil Army was repelled and vanquished.

Then the Evil One switched tactics. Māra summoned his three
daughters Desire, Discontent, and Lust, instructing them to work
the magic of sex and seduce Gotama. Thereupon, the Three Daughters conjured up a host of goddesses skilled in the thirty-two feminine wiles:

> Some of the goddesses veiled only half their faces; some displayed their
> full, round breasts; some teased him with half-smiles of their pearly
> white teeth; some stretched and yawned voluptuously; some puckered
> their ruby-red lips; some gazed at him with sultry eyes; some revealed
> their half-covered breasts; some wore tight or transparent garments
> which showed off the curves of their bodies; some jangled their anklets;
> some festooned their breasts with garlands of flowers; some bared their
> luscious thighs; some paraded around with exotic birds on their heads
> and shoulders; some threw him side-long glances; some deliberately ap-
> peared disheveled; some fingered with their golden girdles; some moved
> enticingly in front of him; some danced and sang; some entreated him
> shamelessly; some swayed their hips like palm trees in the wind; some
> sighed deeply with passion; some strolled about provocatively; some un-
> dressed slowly before him; some revealed their undergarments; some
> walked by him redolent of perfume; some had painted faces and wore
> dangling earrings; some exposed themselves through clever use of their
> garments; some laughed gaily, recounting tales of love play; some dis-
> ported themselves as innocent virgins, others as young brides, and still
> others as mature women; some pleaded with him to satisfy their passion;
> some showered him with fragrant flowers.[32]

The girls sang out:

> It is early spring, the fairest of all seasons!
> All the trees beginning to bud, and flowers to bloom!
> Surely this is the time for pleasure and love,

16

While you are in the prime of your beauty and youth—
Your appearance so graceful, your years so few,
This is the time for you to indulge your desires.
Your present search after supreme wisdom is hard
    to accomplish;
Turn, then, your thoughts from it, and take your pleasure—
Look at us, and behold our beauty and charms—
See our bodies, so perfect in shape, and so fit
    for love,
Our locks so brightly shining, of a rich auburn tint,
Our foreheads broad, and our perfectly shaped heads,
Our eyes so beautifully even and full,
Like the blue lotus flower.
Our noses curved like the beak of a parrot,
Our lips red and shining like rubies,
Resembling the choicest coral in tint; and see our graceful
    necks,
Our teeth so white, and free from disfigurement,
Our tongues so fresh, like the leaf of a lotus flower;
Listen to the soft and charming voices we possess,
    as melodious as that of the gods;
See our bosoms, so enticing, white, and lovely!
Round as the fruit of the pomegranate tree!
See our waists, so lithe and slender, like the handle of the
    bow,
Our buttocks, broad and glossy, placed evenly,
Just as the rounded forehead of the elephant king;
Our flanks, so soft and white, of graceful shape,
Smooth as the trunk of an elephant;
Behold our legs, so round and straight and tapering,
And see how full and plump our feet beneath,
A reddish white in color, like the shining petal
    of the lily.
How beautiful and joy-affording, then, our forms!
Adorned with all these marks of excellence!

Our fingers deft in every kind of music,
Our voices able to produce the softest sounds,
Our feet to dance and give delight to every heart—
What joy even the gods feel to see us thus!
How ravished with the thoughts of love they are!
Why do you not feel the same delight!
Why not covet the same enjoyment!
But like a man who finds a treasury of gold
    and gems,
Leaves all, and goes away far off,
Not knowing the happiness which such wealth can give,
Your heart seems utterly estranged!
You ignore the joys of love and pleasure
And sit, self-absorbed and unmoved—
What a waste!
Why not partake of the world's joys and bliss!
And let nirvana and the path of wisdom be delayed.[33]

When Gotama would not succumb, the Three Daughters tried a different tack: "Men's tastes differ. Instead of sixteen-year-old goddesses, let us assume the shapes of women who have given birth once, women who have given birth twice, women of mature age, and even gray-haired old women."

The effect of all these spectacular enticements, the sweetest a man can be offered, on Gotama was nil. He dismissed them as nothing more than foam and water bubbles, devoid of real substance, pleasure as brief as a flash of lightning or an autumn shower. Gotama said to the Three Daughters, "I am no longer a slave to passions and lust, those razors smeared with honey, which captivate the mind and lead to fever, pain, vexation, and despair. My body is calm and my mind set free."

The Three Daughters gave up in grudging admiration. Any other man, they decided among themselves, would surely have caved in or lost his senses trying to resist such an onslaught.[34]

After withstanding the deadly, all-out assaults of the Demon Army and the Lascivious Three Daughters, Gotama easily handled the rest of Māra's poisoned arrows: Boredom, Hunger and Thirst, Greed, Sloth, Cowardice, Uncertainty, Malice, Obstinacy, and Fame and Glory.

Having completely unburdened himself of all disturbing passions, limiting thoughts, and every other distraction, Gotama was ready one night to encounter Absolute Reality. First he passed through the four stages of meditation: observation and reflection, pure concentration, awakened awareness, and perfect equanimity. Later that night, the inner and outer workings of the universe became clear; then he experienced, intuitively, the entire spectrum of existence; next, after contemplating the origin of cosmic unease and realizing a way to eradicate it, Gotama "knew what is." Upon seeing the morning star, he was a Buddha: "Tranquil in body, with a liberated mind; craving nothing, mindful and detached, calm and unperturbed." One text states that upon Gotama's enlightenment the earth shook like a woman in the throes of bliss—an all-embracing cosmic orgasm that transformed human consciousness.[35]

After abiding in the bliss of nirvana for forty-nine days, Buddha returned to the world to proclaim his message for the welfare of all. He knew from his own experience that wisdom was not communicable, but he hoped to point out the Way for others, helping them create the right recipe for liberation. Buddha taught far and wide until his death at age eighty. His final admonitions were, "Everything decays; train with diligence; rely on yourselves, no one else."

One of the meanings of the word nirvana is "extinguished," and for Gotama Buddha sexual sensation apparently vanished upon his enlightenment, and he could no longer be inflamed by sex. As a prince, Gotama's life was largely centered on sexual indulgence, and as a religious pilgrim, on sexual abstinence; but as a Buddha, both elements were, it seems, transcended. Buddha is portrayed in every text as being totally untroubled by sexual thoughts or feelings throughout his long ministry of forty-five years. He was said to have exclaimed, "All the pleasures known to men, all the pleasures known to the gods, compared to the joy of nirvana are not even a sixteenth part."[36]

As an Awakened One, we are told, his concealed private parts were permanently sheathed, affording no offense or danger to anyone.[37]

19

Soon after his enlightenment, Māra's Three Daughters made one last attempt to ensnare Gotama Buddha. As soon as they appeared before him in the guise of delectable young beauties, however, the voluptuous trio was immediately transformed into wizened old hags. They remained in that state until Buddha magnanimously forgave them and removed the spell. He scolded them, "You cannot test what is beyond being tested." [38] Later in his career, Buddha's rivals would similarly attempt to entrap him with girls, without success, and he would spurn offers from the most powerful kings to wed their daughters. Throughout his life as a teacher, Buddha associated with all types of women, including the most famed courtesans of the time, but treated one and all as "mothers, sisters, or daughters," neither enchanted nor repulsed by members of the opposite sex. Buddha kept his promise and returned to see his Queen Yaśodharā and their son Rāhula. In a marvelous display of pique, Yaśodharā refused to go to the palace gate to greet her ex-husband. "If he really is noble," she told her father-in-law the king, "he will come to *my* presence. Then I shall pay my respects." And, in fact, it was the Buddha who made the first move. [39] Yaśodharā, dressed in bright raiment and jewels, made a final attempt to win Gotama back, but it was too late. According to pious tradition, both Yaśodharā and Rāhula entered the Buddha's Order of Celibates and lived happily ever after. There is, however, other evidence that suggests that Yaśodharā remained aloof, acting as her own refuge, not entirely forgiving Gotama's abrupt abandonment of their marriage bed. [40]

Looking at the story of Gotama in allegorical terms, we can see that it represents ultimates. In the palace, Gotama had access to every kind of physical pleasure (of which sex was preeminent). Such extreme luxury, however, brought him no peace of mind; on the contrary, Gotama discovered that sybaritic indulgence is a deadly narcotic that eventually destroys body and soul. From that extreme, Gotama went to another. All stimulation was shunned and sensual feelings or thoughts ruthlessly suppressed. Shutting out the phenomenal world, depriving oneself of every comfort or enjoyment, and remaining in a state of suspended animation was the goal. This method, too, leads to destruction, as Gotama learned nearly at the cost of his life.

After being immersed in both extremes, Gotama was awakened to the Middle Way, a centered path that leads safely through the poles of all-consuming fiery passion and the frigid depths of ascetic self-torture. While Buddha continued to eat, taking food as medicine, essential for the maintenance of life, sex was entirely dispensed with. Buddha, who had his fill of sex as Gotama the prince, thus represents a state beyond physical craving; *bud* (awake), the root of "Buddha," is neuter, a condition free of both gender and sex. In that respect Buddha ranks infinitely higher than the gods—sooner or later even the delights of paradise corrupt the inhabitants there and they fall again into the whirl of samsara.

Although Buddha's lofty asexuality was held as the ultimate human goal, it was an ideal that few could—or, it must be admitted, would want to—attain, and the problem of sex and how to deal with it remained a sticky issue for each generation of Buddhists.

2

Extinguish the Flames: Sex and the Puritan Elders

One of the Buddha's earliest and most searing discourses was the Fire Sermon: "All is burning . . . burning with the fire of passion, hate, and delusion. When the blaze of passion fades, one is liberated." [1]

Sex, "the blaze of passion," is the primary element of the will to live and the chief expression of craving, the "thirst" that creates the chaos, unease, and suffering that plagues the world. More than anything else, it is the cords of sensuous desire that bind us tighter and tighter to the wheel of life—contact, symbolized by a couple in sexual congress, is the middle link in Buddha's twelve-linked "chain of dependent origin." Sex is a raging fire that scorches and burns, flaring up with intense heat, engulfing the scaffold of self-control and restraint that leads to deliverance.

> Like a moth
> Consumed by a flame,
> Those set ablaze with passion
> Have no refuge. [2]

Tinged with concupiscence, sex is karmically unwholesome, a negative force stirring up an unending flow of wants and needs. Certain Buddhists, who may be described as puritan elders, believed that the only way to achieve lasting peace of mind was to rid oneself of all sexual passion and seek non-attachment. "No matter how intelligent you are, no matter how accomplished you are at meditation, no matter how deep your concentration, if you have not completely conquered sexual passion you have no hope of liberation," they said.[3]

Here is a typical tale from this tradition:

Not long after his enlightenment, Buddha met a large group of young men walking along a road. They asked him, "Reverend Sir, did you see a woman run this way?"

"Why are you looking for her?" Buddha wanted to know.

"We were on a pleasure outing with our wives and brought along a courtesan for our one bachelor friend, but when we were not paying attention she escaped with all our money."

"Which do you think is better," Buddha asked, "seeking a woman or seeking your self?"

When they politely responded, "The self," Buddha sat them down and gave a discourse on the deadly shackles of desire and the value of non-attachment. Convinced, the young men renounced the world and joined the Order of Celibates.[4]

The puritan Buddha warned his monks, "The one thing that enslaves a man above all else is a woman. Her form, her voice, her scent, her attractiveness, and her touch all beguile a man's heart. Stay away from them at all costs." [5]

Once a monk was meditating in a remote grove. A courtesan who was waiting for an assignation happened to be nearby, and when her customer failed to appear she decided to tempt the monk instead, performing a striptease. The monk became "suffused with excitement," but Buddha came to the rescue. Appearing in the form of a vision, Buddha reminded the monk, "Brother, there is no real delight in passion; real delight is to be free of passion." [6]

Yet many of Buddha's followers were unable to give up what they loved best: "How can we turn away from those who are beautiful in form and inviting to the touch, with every part delightful and so pleasing to behold? How can we reject them when they give us enticing glances and captivate our hearts?" [7] Others insisted, "Happiness is found in the soft arms of a young woman." [8]

To cure such addiction to the pleasures of the flesh, Buddhist texts prescribe a number of remedies, the most effective being meditation on the loathsomeness of the body, a device Gotama used to good effect when he himself was enticed by Māra's daughters.

23

Oh handsome one! Our faces are as bright as the moon.
Look at us, radiant as a lotus flower.
Behold our faultless white teeth,
There is no one to rival us in heaven and on earth—
Come, come, take the prize and shun us not.
Become one with us! [9]

Buddha coolly responded:

Beautiful you may seem,
But from the crown of your heads
To the soles of your feet
You are nothing more than bags of skin
Filled with blood, pus, and filth. [10]

Imagine yourself, Buddha was said to have instructed certain people,[11] in a charnel ground scattered with corpses: some swollen and blackened with decomposition; some pecked at by crows, ravens, and vultures and gnawed by dogs and jackals; some stripped of flesh; and some rotted away to dust. The body is really just an ulcer with nine gaping wounds filled with various mean impurities. Even the loveliest woman and the handsomest man will someday age into tottering old wrecks, wrinkled, bald, toothless, with blotchy skin, and then enter the grave. Be always mindful of the body's impermanence and corruptibility, and turn away from the enslaving pleasure of the senses; then you will be capable of experiencing a pure form of rapture untainted by desire or clinging. Indeed, the joy of being released from craving is ten times more delightful than all the pleasures of the world rolled into one.

On occasion, even more bitter medicine for lovesick and backsliding disciples was ordered, as in this gruesome tale:

Srima, the loveliest courtesan of Rājagaha, generously served the finest of food to Buddhist mendicants on their daily rounds. A young monk fell madly in love with her at first sight, and when he returned to the monastery he pined away for her, refusing to eat. That night the courtesan suddenly died.

Buddha ordered that the body of Srima not be cremated, but rather placed outside in the charnel ground. He gave instructions that the corpse be guarded so it would not be devoured by wild animals. By the fourth day the body, infected with maggots, began to bloat and ooze. Then Buddha had the king summon the townsfolk to have a last look at Srimā.

When the crowd assembled around the decaying corpse, Buddha called out, "Who will pay one thousand gold coins [which was formerly her customary fee] to spend the night with Srimā? Five hundred? Two hundred? One hundred? Fifty? Ten? One? A single penny?"

There were no takers.

The lovesick monk, in the meantime, had turned deathly pale and retched at the sight. Buddha concluded, "Behold this body disfigured and corrupt, a vile mass of sores and maggots, now despised. Nothing is stable, nothing remains." [12]

Again and again, the theme of the body's imperfection and corruptibility is hammered home by the puritan Buddhists. Here is a rather poetic elaboration of the precariousness of human existence and the loathsomeness of the body, by the Japanese monk Kūkai:

> The loveliest maiden eventually disappears in the depths of the earth, and even an emperor one day perishes like smoke. The delicate eyebrows of a beautiful woman vanish like mist, and her once sparkling teeth rot, no more permanent than dew. Sooner or later, the eyes of the most exquisite girl become small swamps and her ears empty holes for the wind to blow through. Her pink cheeks become a feast for flies, and her luscious lips food for crows. Her once-enchanting smile can no longer be seen on a weatherbeaten skeleton. Alive, she may have been the most sought-after of women; dead, no one will even go near her decayed corpse. Her lovely black hair is tangled among weeds and her graceful arms are covered with mold. Her sweet fragrance has been carried away forever by the wind. [13]

For a woman excessively attached to her appearance, Buddha conjured up a maid lovelier than any mortal could imagine. "Look at her," Buddha told the vain woman as he caused the beautiful phantom to age while they watched—first a sixteen-year-old virgin, then a twenty-year-old bride, next a young mother, a mature matron, a decrepit old woman, and, finally, a festering corpse oozing pus, covered with worms, and torn at by crows and jackals.

25

"Behold the emptiness of externals; do not cling to the body, a bag of bones plastered with flesh and blood." [14]

Although it relates equally harsh tactics, the following tale has a slightly more positive ending.

A depraved courtesan heard that a particular monk was especially goodlooking, but he spurned her repeated invitations to come and give instruction in the teachings of Buddhism. The courtesan murdered one of her patrons, and was found out. Condemned to death by dismemberment, the courtesan was impaled on a stake. After her hands, feet, nose, and ears had been sliced off, the monk showed up. "Why didn't you come visit me when I was still beautiful?" she cried out in agony. "Before, I would surely have been tempted by your great beauty," the monk said honestly. He then delivered a discourse on the law of impermanence, a reality the courtesan now understood only too well. With her dying breath, we are happy to learn, the courtesan attained the "pure eye of the Dharma" and was assured of eventual salvation. [15]

One of the favorite ploys of Māra, the Evil One, was to transform himself into a stunning beauty whenever Buddha or one of his senior monks addressed a crowd of men. When the lascivious creature distracted everyone's attention, the Buddhists got it back by turning the temptress into a dreadful skeleton. [16] Similarly, a monk was once confronted by a gorgeous stripper. After she had removed all her clothes, he demanded, "Now take off your skin!" [17]

Even the shock-treatment approach [18] did not work with those truly smitten. Buddha's half-brother, the handsome Nanda, ignored all the master's admonitions on the perils of sexual entanglement, remaining hopelessly infatuated with his bride-to-be. Buddha, concerned for his brother's eternal salvation, had, in effect, Nanda kidnapped before the wedding could take place. Though others may have flocked to the Order of Celibates, Nanda wanted no part of it and tried to escape from the clutches of his brother's loyal followers. Finally Buddha transported Nanda magically to Indra's heaven and introduced him to the nymphs of paradise. Nanda had to admit that his fiancée was no match for these celestial maids. "How do I get reborn here?" he asked. Buddha informed him that such enticing delights were reserved for those who behaved best. In hope of meeting the breathtakingly beautiful damsels again, Nanda resigned himself to the religious life. Eventually, we are told, Nanda, the "lover of the nymphs," overcame his vain fascination with feminine beauty, earthly and heavenly, and became an exemplary monk.[19]

Once a virtuous monk died during meditation, and he was rewarded by being reborn in paradise. When he was welcomed by a host of celestial maidens, he cried out, "I don't want this! I want nirvana!"[20]

The puritan Buddha is sometimes portrayed as being more in sympathy with the predicament of "passion-tossed" monks. Once a brother fell hopelessly in love with a woman of surpassing beauty whom he encountered on his begging rounds. She occupied his every thought, and, "pierced with love's shafts and sick with desire," he began wasting away. His fellow monks berated him unmercifully:

"Once you were calm in mind and serene of countenance, but now look at you! It is a great privilege to be able to hear and practice the Buddhist Law as a member of the Order, so why have you succumbed to sexual longing? Such base passion brings nothing but misery and despair, and it will eventually destroy you. We thought you knew that!"

The smitten monk may have known that, but his lovesickness nevertheless persisted, and he was taken before the Buddha.

Buddha, hearing the monk's plight, commiserated with him. "You may be under the sway of intense longing right now, but if you can check your thoughts and keep in mind your noble mission, the passions will cool, and you will not be guilty of improper conduct." Buddha then related this tale of a previous incarnation:

"I was a king, and in my domain there was a maid as lovely as a celestial nymph—she intoxicated every man who looked upon her. The first time I saw her I became mad with passion, even though she was the wife of my faithful commander in chief. I lay on my royal couch, unable to sleep night or day, and sighed:

> When will this slender-waisted maid,
> With rich, full breasts,
> Embrace me with her soft arms
> And cling to me as tightly as a vine?"

The commander in chief generously offered to present his wife to the king to prevent his lord's demise from lovesickness; fortunately the king, reminded of his sacred duties toward his realm, snapped out of his love stupor and rid himself of his infatuation—the moral of the story being that the monk should do the same.[21]

In a related tale, Buddha told of living as a yogin, proud of his mastery of mind and body. The king of the province in which the yogin resided was impressed by the ascetic's apparent self control and took the yogin as his personal guru. One day when the king was absent, the queen come down to make the daily offering of food. Freshly bathed and adorned, she accidentally slipped out of her robe when she rose to greet him. The yogin was inflamed with desire, and "the cobra of evil passion" welled up within him. In a swoon, the yogin stumbled out of the palace. All he could think of for the next week was, "What a woman! What lovely hands and feet! Her full breasts, her luscious hips and thighs! How I want her!" In one version of the story, the yogin actually succumbs to the queen's charms and makes passionate love to her prior to being shamed out of his bad behavior by the return of the king. In the end, the yogin returns to the safety of the Himalayas, remote from the deadly temptations of the world.[22]

Women, the puritan Buddha warns elsewhere, are never to be trusted. In a previous incarnation, the Buddha-to-be enjoyed the services of the town's chief courtesan every day, rewarding her with a thousand gold coins each time. One day he forgot to bring along his purse, and the courtesan had him thrown out—despite the fact that he had given her a fortune over the years. Declaring that women are ungrateful and treacherous, he renounced the world and sought a haven deep in the forest.[23]

Even in a mountain sanctuary one has to be careful. An ascetic acquired a son in a most unusual manner: While bathing in a stream he emitted some semen into the water. The semen mixed with the water and was swallowed by a doe, who miraculously conceived. The resultant boy-child was raised by the ascetic in the mountains and grew up unaware that females existed. To make a long story short, a girl from the city was sent to seduce the boy. After the boy innocently invited her into the hermitage, the girl showed him her "wound."

"A wild animal clawed off my organ," she explained. "The wound is very deep and itches terribly. If you want to help me, I'll show you the best way to scratch it." When the boy's father returned just after the girl had departed, he asked why none of the chores had been done. "Another boy, with the most unusual body, visited me. He taught me how to play doctor and other games. I enjoyed myself so much I forgot all about my duties." The father explained the facts of life to the boy and made him promise never to do that again, for sex is anathema to an ascetic.[24]

Other Buddhist stories in this vein are simple morality tales. When the ravishing beauty Queen Ubbarī died, the inconsolable king had her body embalmed in oil and placed in his room. The king assumed that his queen had gone to the Abode of the Celestials, but when he questioned Buddha about this he was told, "No, she has been reborn as a female dung beetle because of her extreme vanity. During her time on earth all she did was beautify herself and indulge in sensuality, failing to perform meritorious acts, give alms, and observe the moral precepts. Her haughty, vainglorious behavior landed her in an inferior birth."

The king refused to believe this, so Buddha brought forth the dung beetle and had her speak: "Yes, I was your queen, but now I am the mate of the dung beetle in front of me. I love and follow him everywhere." The king had her body disposed of the next day.[25]

In a similar tale, Queen Mallikā misbehaved with her pet dog one day in her bathhouse. The king inadvertently witnessed the scene, but the clever queen was able to convince him that it was really an optical illusion created by steam and shadows. The queen died, and the king went to Buddha to ask the location of her rebirth. The queen, in fact, had fallen into hell for the twin sins of bestiality and deceit, but rather than give him a straight answer Buddha used his occult powers to make the king forget the reason for his visits. After a week of paying her karmic debt in hell, the queen was reborn in the Abode of the Celestials, for other than the lapse with the dog, she had been a good Buddhist. This time Buddha let the king ask his question and gave him a truthful answer.[26]

Sex can be very dangerous. Buddha one morning on his begging rounds noticed a lively group of local princes, decked out in all their youthful splendor, leaving for an outing at the pleasure park. A fight broke out among the young men over a particularly attractive girl, and in the ensuing altercation they nearly beat one another to death. Buddha saw them being returned to the city, beaten and bloody, on stretchers. "For a single woman they have come to this. From lust springs grief. . . . " [27]

Once a monk inadvertently entered a woman's bedchamber. When he noticed a woman asleep naked on the bed, he beat a hasty retreat. Unfortunately, he ran into the woman's husband at the door. The monk, naturally suspected of the worst, was given a sound thrashing. Buddha's advice to all mendicants: "Watch your step!" [28]

Then there is this fable warning of the risks involved with wanton behavior: A monkey, symbol of uncontrollable animal passion, once entered the hermitage of a meditating sage and stuck its penis into the sage's ear, the closest available orifice. The sage, deep in meditation, did not flinch. Later, though, the monkey stuck its member into the mouth of a napping snapping turtle sunning itself on a rock. When it realized what was happening, the turtle clamped down and withdrew into its shell. Shrieking with pain, the monkey went to the sage and pleaded, "Please help me! I promise never to be bad again!" After reproaching the monkey for its shameful behavior, the sage persuaded the turtle to let go. The monkey wisely reformed. [29]

Some puritan tales describe the encumbrances of married life. The craving for sex, lovers, and children is likened to heavy fetters, a thousand times stronger than those of iron; those who are wise leave all love and desire behind.

Once a young hermit fell in love with a plump miss who enticed him from his master. "You may go, my son," the master told him, "but do not forget the peace and quiet you enjoyed in this hermitage." No sooner had the young man taken the girl to wife than she began ordering him around, and he was sent scurrying to and fro for every little thing she needed. Rushing about in a ceaseless round of errands and chores, the young man thought, "I am no better than her slave!" Worn out, he left his wife and returned, shamefaced, to this master. "I was happy here until I met that shrewish woman. She drove me crazy with her endless demands. I am glad to be back." [30]

Women who became Buddhist nuns often shared similar sentiments toward loutish husbands, intolerable mothers-in-law, ungrateful children, and the presumed joys of married life. Sumedhā shaved off her hair to protest her arranged engagement to the king, then lectured her would-be husband on the futility of worldly life— "With a chance for nirvana, what need is there for sensual pleasure, that raging fire? Delight in the senses will burn you badly!"—before running off to join the Order of Celibates.[31]

One nun told a horrific story to a group of nuns who had joined the Order en masse following the death of their husbands in war. The young nuns were having difficulty with the vow of celibacy; "grabbed by desire," they still felt attracted to the pleasures of sex. The nun told them, "I was traveling with my husband and our two children. When I awoke one morning, I found my husband dead from a snake bite; the body had already begun to decompose. After burying him I quickly headed home, but I lost the two children— one swept away in a river and the other devoured by a wolf. When I arrived at my family home, I was told that my parents and the rest of my relatives had perished in a fire. I married again, but my second husband was a drunk. When our baby was born, he fell into a drunken rage and forced me to kill and eat the infant. He died shortly thereafter, and I was, according to the local custom, buried alive with the body. A grave robber found me and took me as his concubine. He was caught and executed, and once again I was entombed with a corpse. I was saved when a wolf dug up the grave. Finally I met the Buddha and joined the Order of Nuns."

Not surprisingly, upon hearing this dreadful tale of woe the young nuns were forever cured of any desire to return to the married state.[32]

Generally, it was the men who left their wives and ran off to join the Order, but there is mention of the tables being turned. When one husband announced his intention of becoming a monk, the wife countered, "That has been my wish for years." Under a pretext, she was able to get out of the house before he could leave, and it was she that became ordained, saddling her husband with the responsibility of raising the kids! (The woman was criticized, however, for abandoning her children without first having taught her husband how to cook properly.)[33]

Some well-matched couples renounced the world together. Mahākāssapa, for instance, was forced by his parents to marry. However, his bride was also a convert to puritan Buddhism, so they took a mutual vow of celibacy. They placed a garland of flowers between them at night as a reminder of the vow. Eventually, they were able to formally join the Order of Celibates.[34]

At the beginning, the Order of Celibates was small in number, and the fresh converts were devoted to the Buddha and his teaching. Trouble arose eventually, however, forcing Buddha to implement rules. And the first rule, human beings what they are, concerned sex.

Sudinna, the only son of a rich merchant, had renounced the world and joined the Order of Celibates. One day Sudinna passed by his former home. His parents came out and pleaded with him not to leave them without an heir, the greatest tragedy that could befall an Indian family. Sudinna refused to rejoin his former wife, but when she was brought to him by his mother in the woods where he was staying, dressed in what had been his favorite of her outfits and ready for love, he succumbed and had intercourse with her three times. Sudinna seemed to have enjoyed the interlude at the time, judging by the frequency of their embrace. But later, struck with remorse, he confessed to Buddha.

Buddha then pronounced these harshest of words: "It is better that your penis enter the mouth of a hideous cobra or a pit of blazing coals than enter a woman's vagina." A rule was made that henceforth a monk who indulged in any type of sexual intercourse was "defeated" and no longer in communion;[35] sexual intercourse negates one's ordination and is a thing that must not be done "as long as life lasts."[36] The hapless Sudinna was spared expulsion because his transgression occurred before there was a rule against it! (Incidentally, Sudinna's wife conceived—his mother had cleverly waited until her daughter-in-law was fertile. It is said that both Sudinna's ex-wife and the son born to her later entered the Order.)

The *Vinaya,* the huge rule book for the Order of Celibates that developed from this and subsequent episodes, contains a compendium of sex and sexual misbehavior.[37] The second entry after the Sudinna case concerns a monk who kept a female monkey for bestial purposes. He was found out when the monkey approached a group of monks and meekly bent over, waiting to be entered.

These monks spied on the monkey's owner and witnessed him first sharing his almsfood with the monkey and then mounting his sex-pet. When challenged, the monk retorted that Buddha's rule applied only to women and not to female animals. Buddha was informed, denounced the monk's actions, and amended the rule to include sexual intercourse with an animal.[38]

In the next entry, a group of rowdy monks at Vesālī was censured for eating, drinking, bathing as much as they liked, and, on top of everything else, indulging in sexual intercourse. They begged to be forgiven, pleading, "We were harming no others, only ourselves," but Buddha did not buy that argument and they were booted out.[39]

The rule book then goes on to state that if a monk's penis enters any orifice of a human being (female, male, hermaphrodite, or eunuch), a nonhuman (demon or ghost), or an animal, even if the penetration is only the length of a sesame seed, it is grounds for expulsion. Nor can the rule be circumvented by fucking someone or something that is asleep, drunk, mad, or dead, that is, unconscious of the fact. If a monk, for example, has any kind of intercourse with a sleeping brother, he is always to be expelled; judgment on the other party depends on whether or not be consented either before or after the act.[40]

The rest of the first section of the *Vinaya* contains a truly bizarre (not to mention ingenious) list of examples of sexual indiscretions and outright perversion by members of the supposed Order of Celibates. Here is a sample: brothers who disguised themselves in elaborate costumes to hide their identity as monks when they transgressed; monks who committed incest with their mothers, daughters, or sisters; an acrobatic monk who performed fellatio on himself; a monk with such a long penis that he could be his own sodomist; monks who fucked, respectively, an open sore on a dead body, a plaster decoration, a wooden doll, corpses in various stages of decomposition, a severed head, the bones of a dead lover, a dragon-maiden, a fairy, a ghost, and a doe. (It should be noted that the above list consists only of those acts confessed to by remorseful monks or accounts of those who were found out.) A monk whose sex organs were "impaired" thought he would be free from the rule against intercourse because he had no sensation; he was wrong and got the heave-ho. A monk who succumbed to ordinary seduction was defeated regardless of whether his role in the sex act was passive, active, or nonpenetrating (merely spraying the women with semen).[41]

There was, however, an exception made in the case of the pious laywomen Supabbā and Saddhā. Both are described as loyal followers of the Enlightened One, and both held the view that the highest gift a woman can give is sex. They offered that gift taking full responsibility for the act (which evidently did not involve penetration), and the lucky monks on the receiving end escaped with the lesser punishment of a formal summons before the community (usually resulting in probation and a suitable penance).[42]

That is the same punishment meted out to a monk who arranged to have intercourse with a woman but became conscience-stricken at the initial touch.[43] More puzzling is the application of that lesser penalty to a perverted monk who used his thumb to penetrate a young girl who subsequently died (from what, we are not informed).[44]

No offense is involved with a nun who is raped, a monk who is attacked by a woman but resists, monks or nuns forced into sex acts by outside parties, or monks who just dream about having intercourse with ex-wives or lovers.[45]

There is a long section recounting incidents in which a monk drifted off to sleep, had an involuntary erection, and then was mounted by women passers-by. One monk with a particularly rigid erection was mounted by a group of perfume girls, who then praised him as a bull of a man. After he awoke, other monks noticed the huge stain on his robe and reported him, but he was not punished, because he had been asleep during the entire affair. Buddha, however, cautioned monks to keep their doors closed when sleeping to prevent such occurrences.[46]

The second section of the *Vinaya* concerns the prohibition against "taking what is not given," that is, stealing. Most of the entries deal with theft of food and possessions. One hapless monk found a large chunk of pork floating in a stream he was crossing. When he dutifully returned the meat to the butcher who had lost it, he was mistakenly accused of stealing it. Believing himself to be automatically expelled from the Order, the monk accepted a woman cowherd's invitation to sport. The two incidents were reported to Buddha, and he declared, "The monk was innocent of theft but guilty of sexual misconduct, so he must be dimissed." [47]

The *Vinaya*'s third section takes up the prohibition against depriving a being of life. In one entry, a group of dastardly monks lusted after the wife of a lay follower. They extolled the pleasures of the extravagant rewards the man would receive in heaven because of his good deeds in this life and enticed him to sample those delights without delay. The layman fell for it and soon ate and drank himself to death. His outraged widow learned of the plot and denounced the monks to Buddha. They were judged guilty of murder and ousted from the Order.[48] Monks who provided abortifacients to pregnant women were condemned as murderers and expelled.[49] Monks who prepared fertility or contraceptive medicines that resulted in the death of the women involved were subject to the lesser charge of "wrong doing." [50]

The next section on defeat in the *Vinaya* covers the telling of lies and contains few references to sex. The following section, however, on offenses requiring a summons before a formal meeting of the Order, is full of sexual escapades and anecdotes. Like section one, the opening entry in this section also pertains to sex: A tiresome monk named Seyyasaka had great difficulty with the rule of celibacy. His sexual frustration had made him thin and wretched, yellow-skinned and purple-veined. A worldly elder monk told him, "You look terrible. If you want to get better, eat, drink, and sleep as much as you want and masturbate to relieve sexual pressure." Seyyasaka wholeheartedly followed the elder's advice and within a short time was a new man, with a bright complexion and clear skin. When the other monks asked the reason for his amazing recovery, Seyyasaka revealed the secret. Instead of embarking on a similar health plan, however, the monks asked with distaste, "Do you eat with the same hand you use to masturbate?"

"Of course," Seyyasaka beamed.

The monks tattled on Seyyasaka, and he was brought before Buddha. Seyyasaka was given a stern lecture on the absolute necessity of a monk's being passionless and devoid of all fetters. The errant monk was not expelled, but he did have to appear before the Order and be disciplined.[51]

Thereafter, with the exception of those who had wet dreams and totally involuntary emission, anyone who ejaculated was guilty of wrongdoing and had to appear before the Order.

A curious cataloguing of the various kinds of ejaculation then appears in the *Vinaya*.[52] There are emissions brought about by self-stimulation, external stimulation, and by a combination of both internal and external stimulation; by simulated intercourse (moving the hips up and down in the air, for example), by a fit of sexual passion, by the pressure of defecation and/or urination, by wind blowing on the penis, and by the swelling accompanying the bite of an *uccalinga* bug; for reasons of health (as in Seyyasaka's case), for physical pleasure, and for use as a medicine; as a donation, as a "virtuous act," as a religious sacrifice, as a means of attaining heavenly bliss, as a means of fertilizing an egg, and as an experiment to see if one can ejaculate the ten kinds of semen (black, yellow, red, white, *takka*-colored, aqua, oily, milky, creamy, and frothy); and for amusement. All such intentional emissions are transgressions requiring a formal summons before the Order. There is no offense, however, if the monk is dreaming, is unhinged, insane, or suffering from a disease, or is a novice.

The remainder of this section discusses the problem of intentional and unintentional ejaculation. If the emission is intentional, the monk is to be disciplined; if involuntary—caused by a dream or a sudden fit of sexual passion, or for physiological reasons and the like—it is not an offense. It all depends on intent. If, for example, a monk fondles his testicles and ejaculates on purpose it is an offense; if he touches them inadvertently, as, for instance, in the bath and emits semen he is not charged.

This part of the text goes on to describe monks who ejaculated while bathing, aroused to do so by the warmth of the room, the spray of water, or the erotic experience or washing the back of their master. Creative methods of masturbation are also touched upon: pressing against one's bladder while urinating; applying hot compresses to the penis; holding a sleeping novice's penis in one hand while yanking one's own with the other; asking a novice monk to manually stimulate one's penis; fantasizing about a woman's vagina; and sticking one's penis into a keyhole, a bunch of flowers, mud, sand, or water.

The second portion in this section takes up a host of issues related to sex. A brahmin and his wife once paid a visit to the renowned monastery of a monk called Udāyin. The couple was invited in for a closer look. While the husband was admiring the austere beauty of the monk's cell, Udāyin was admiring the man's wife, repeatedly rubbing his body against hers from behind. When the couple left the premises, the husband praised the monk, but the wife rejoined, "There is nothing noble about that lecher. He kept pressing against me the entire time we were in his cell."

The brahmin was naturally upset and spread the word that Buddhist monks were shameless, immoral liars. Informed of the matter, Udāyin was summoned and given the standard lecture on the necessity of a monk's being able to still, and above all control the passions. Buddha declared it an offense to have any bodily contact with a woman. Due to circumstances that arose, the rule was expanded to include improper physical contact with men, eunuchs, and animals as well. It was even an offense for a monk to touch his own mother, sister, or daughter, albeit to a lesser degree. More serious was touching one's former wife, women who are sleeping, unconscious, or dead, and any type of flirting. There were also rules against clothing fetishism and transvestism.[53]

In the next part of the *Vinaya*, Udāyin again misbehaves. This time he talks about sex and tells dirty stories with a group of women visiting his monastery. Udāyin is reported and then reprimanded (but not punished, because the act was committed before there was a rule against it). Thereafter, it was an offense to use lewd language. The only exceptions were if the language served the higher purpose of explaining the Dharma or if the monk was insane.[54]

Then we are treated to examples of double-entendres employed by licentious monks with unsuspecting women. For example: A monk said to a woman farmer, "Well, sister, looks like you have been doing some sowing."

"Yes, honored sir," the woman replied innocently, "but I still haven't closed the furrow."[55]

In the next section, Udāyin—the archetypal bad monk—becomes more blatant. He impresses a beautiful young widow with a wonderful discourse on the Dharma. Wishing to thank him somehow, the widow asks him what sort of alms he needs.

Udāyin tells her, "What is hard to come by for monks."

"What is that, honored sir?" the widow inquires, so she can offer it to him.

"Sexual intercourse."

"If that will be of use, I will present it to you," she said and went inside to disrobe.

Udāyin approached the naked widow, but then for some perverse reason cried out, "Who would want to touch this evil-smelling wench!" He spat, and stormed from the room.

The young widow was furious. "Who does that sham monk think he is? He begs me to have intercourse with him and then has the nerve to call me an evil-smelling wench. What evil have I done? To whom am I inferior in beauty?"

This unpleasant incident resulted in another rule making it an offense to attempt seduction of a woman by convincing her that sex is a suitable offering. Despite the rule, however, a number of monks continued to try to do so, as can be seen by the subsequent list of offenders pleading for the offering of "the highest gift." [56]

Udāyin further figures prominently in other sex sagas. He acts as a go-between, talking a courtesan he knows into giving her daughter in marriage to the son of one of his patrons. The courtesan unwisely entrusts her daughter to Udāyin, and after the girl's marriage to the boy she is treated like a slave and begs to return home. A scandal ensues, and Udāyin is called on the carpet once more. "No matchmaking by monks," is the outcome. [57]

Udāyin persists, though, next serving as pimp for a bunch of fellows he knows. The courtesan they want refuses because she does not know them. They decide to ask Udāyin to procure her for them, betting among themselves on his answer. (Those who thought that he would agree had a safe bet.) Of course, Udāyin is found out, and this time "No pimping by monks," is the decree. [58]

In another story, Udāyin visits a girl he knows just after her marriage and sits with her, out of the sight of others, in an inner room. Although nothing untoward occurred on this occasion, when told of the matter Buddha issued a prohibition against monks being alone with a woman for any reason. [59]

Udāyin's ex-wife joined the Order as a nun, and the two frequently met. They dressed together sometimes, and one day after flashing their private parts, the excited Udāyin ejaculated on his robe. The nun tried to remove the stain by dabbing it with her tongue and then unwisely wiping off the robe between her legs. Pregnant as a result, she blamed it all on Udāyin, who was faulted not for impregnating his ex-wife but for not washing his own robe! [60]

In other sections of the *Vinaya,* Udāyin is taken to task for making robes for nuns (evidently he was a skilled tailor) and teaching women the Dharma in the privacy of their own rooms. [61]

Nothing seemed beneath certain monks in the Order. One group was disgruntled because they were unable to eat their fill at a rich layman's home, a situation they attributed to the elder Dabba, leader of a rival faction. They conspired to have Dabba expelled from the Order and persuaded a nun to accuse him of rape. Fortunately, the truth came out—Dabba told Buddha, "From the time I was born, I cannot recall a single instance in which I wanted to engage in sexual intercourse, not even in a dream"—and the guilty monks were punished. In a related tale, monks jealous of the elder's virginity named a randy billy goat "Dabba." When Buddha found out, those monks were severely rebuked for such defamation. [62]

There were monks who took their vows seriously. While on a journey, Anuruddha requested lodging at a rest-house in a certain village. The woman proprietress welcomed him, but soon after he was taken in a group arrived and also asked to be put up.

The proprietress became enamored of the handsome monk and invited him to spend the night in her quarters on the pretense that the rest-house would be too crowded and noisy for him. Anuruddha consented, and the woman moved quickly to prepare the chamber. She set up a luxurious couch and dressed herself in her most alluring clothes and wore her sweetest perfume. When Anuruddha entered, she declared her love for him and added that they would make a perfect couple. She cast off her gown and paraded before the monk. But even when she slipped onto the couch next to him, Anuruddha admirably retained control of his faculties and successfully resisted the woman's considerable charms.

Amazed at the monk's dignified self-control, the woman asked for forgiveness, listened keenly to the monk's Dharma discourse through the rest of the night, and that morning took refuge in the Buddha's teaching. Word got out about the episode, and Anuruddha was, rather surprisingly, censured despite his noble behavior and conversion of the woman—he had allowed himself to be alone with a woman in her sleeping quarters, and that is absolutely forbidden.[63]

There was once a divinely handsome monk nicknamed "Ocean of Beauty." Over the fierce opposition of his parents, he joined the Order of Celibates. A courtesan offered, for a suitable price, to persuade Ocean of Beauty to return to the world.

She started out by renting a house along Ocean of Beauty's regular mendicant route. Each day she prepared increasingly delicious fare for the monk. Finally she was able to lure him inside and thereupon apply the ways in which a woman can accost a man:

> by yawning, by bowing down, by making amorous gestures, by pretending to be abashed, by rubbing the nails of one hand or foot with the nails of the other hand or foot, by scratching words on the ground with a stick; by causing the man to leap up, by causing him to jump down, by dallying with him, by making him dally with her, by kissing him, by making him kiss her, by eating food, by making him eat food, by giving, by asking for gifts, by imitating whatever he does; by talking in loud tones, by talking in low tones; by talking with him in public, by talking with him in private; by dancing, by singing, by playing musical instruments, by weeping, by adorning herself, by laughing, by gazing; by swaying her hips, by displaying her undergarments, by showing her breasts, by showing her armpits, by showing her navel; by winking, by lifting an eyebrow, by touching her lips, by licking her tongue; by removing her panties, by taking off her headdress, and by putting on her headdress.

Then she said to him, "We are young and meant for each other; let us retire from the world later on when we are old and gray."

Ocean of Beauty had not put up much of a fight until the last moment. He suddenly reaffirmed his vows to himself and escaped from the woman's clutches. Buddha praised him by repeating the familiar litany, "Monks, there is no real delight in passion; real delight is to be free of passion." [64]

More extreme is the story of a monk who maintained his vow of celibacy at the cost of his life. A sixteen-year-old girl—in Buddhist literature, the ultimate temptation for a male—had her eye on a handsome monk and used a pretense to lure him inside her home. She pleaded with him to satisfy her desire. Sorely tempted, the preaching the destruction of the human race," because of wholesale conversions to Buddhist monasticism, and he therefore hoped to limit the number of celibates.

At any rate, the Order of Nuns was founded, [70] and the original rules for them were even more exacting than those for monks. [71] A candidate had, first of all, to prove that she was a woman by passing a discreet gynecological exam and then wait to be ordained to ensure that she was not pregnant.

This rule was initiated following the episode of Uppala the Pregnant Nun. Her parents had forced Uppala to marry against her wishes. After hearing her graphic lecture on the loathsomeness of the body, Uppala's husband told her, "If that is how you feel about it then you will be better off as a nun." Uppala was admitted to the Order but soon displayed unmistakable signs of pregnancy. Accused of transgressing her vows, Uppala insisted that she was innocent. To settle the dispute, Buddha had Uppala examined by an experienced midwife, who determined that the nun had conceived the child while still married. Uppala was allowed to remain in the Order. (She had the baby and nursed it for several months in the nunnery before it was adopted.) [72]

Following ordination, a nun was subject to immediate expulsion if she was willingly penetrated in any orifice by the depth of a sesame seed, and she was strictly prohibited from having any kind of contact with a male. [73] She must be decently clothed at all times, even when bathing. This rule was instituted when a group of nuns happened to bathe in a river with some pleasure girls. "What is the use of giving up sex when you are still young and pretty?" the pleasure girls asked. "Take a vow of chastity when you are old and gray. Then you can have it both ways." The nuns were "confused" by that persuasive argument and reported back to Buddha. "Life is impermanent and you may be dead tomorrow," Buddha reminded them, and then added, "Wear bathing gowns from now on." [74]

Here is an alternate explanation for the bathing gown rule. One day a group of five men caught sight of a bathing nun and stared at her. She asked them, "Why do you want to look at this vile, smelly bag of filth?" "That's not what we see," the young men replied. When they refused to go away, the nun came out of the water to leave, and the men fell into a frenzy. She managed to escape, and when Buddha was informed of the incident he made the wearing of monk braced himself by recalling the sterling examples of illustrious monks. Convinced that he had no escape—even if he resisted the girl's advances he still could falsely be charged with rape[65]—the monk asked the girl to wait a few moments. He entered the bathroom, found a razor, and slit his throat. The monk was praised as a virgin martyr to the Buddhist cause.[66]

A female virgin martyr was the nun Subha. She was beautiful even with a shorn head and in a robe of rags. Once she was accosted by a handsome young man who pleaded with her, "Don't waste your life wearing that dirty old robe. You are as lovely as a nymph, as radiant as an angel, and your eyes enthrall me. Let me clothe you with the finest silk and adorn your lovely body with delightful fragrances and precious garlands. Join me so that we can make love continually on a luxurious couch." She rebuffed him with these words: "This body which attracts you so is in reality a bag of filth. Sexual passion will destroy you, and it is something which I have overcome." Still, the young man persisted in his advances. The nun then plucked out her eye and said, "Here, take this since you like it so much." [67]

A much milder version of this "celibacy as sanctity" theme is found in Japan. A devout Buddhist laywoman, with her husband's permission, made a vow of chastity. That is more easily said than done, as puritan Buddhists have discovered over the centuries, and she was plagued by erotic desires. An itinerant priest, learning of her plight, carved a naked image of Amida Buddha for her. That same night a Bodhisattva appeared to her and said, "When you are agitated by desire pray to that Buddha. Soon you will no longer be troubled." Although it seems incongruous that praying to a naked statue is the best way to cure addiction to sex, the moral is that one should return to a state of childlike purity in which there is nothing shameful about the body.[68]

The Order of Nuns was established sometime after the Order of Monks. Buddha was reported to be very reluctant to form a group for women, perhaps fearing that they would be even harder to control than his horde of horny monks, and that the two groups would get into mischief with each other. (He was right. From the beginning monks were reported as having sexually harassed the nuns. No doubt, too, he was aware of the criticism that "Gotama a bathing gown obligatory. He also explained why the five young men became so inflamed with passion. In a previous incarnation, the men were five celestials who lusted after a young maiden. They decided among themselves that the one who displayed the greatest passion should have her.

The first god said, "My passion is so great that I cannot sit still." The second said, "My passion is so great that I want to charge like an army." The third said, "My passion is so great that I am like a log racing out of control down a river." The fourth said, "My passion is so great that I am like a horsefly that never stops buzzing." The fifth concluded, "My passion is so great that I do not know whether I am alive or dead." The fifth god was declared the most passionate and was presented with the maid, who was in fact the nun in a previous life. (This kind of erotically tinged digression is quite common in puritan Buddhist texts, indicating a still-keen interest in the pleasures of the flesh.)[75]

Masturbation was condemned—when taking a bath and washing one's private parts, the fingers could not be inserted into the vagina past the first knuckle—and the nuns were warned not to resort to the use of dildoes, including vegetables.[76]

As mentioned above, nuns were not held responsible in cases of rape. One nun in singularly deep meditation was violated without being aware of it, noticing the evidence only after she came out of her trance. Although not subject to punishment, she was admonished to find a safer place in which to practice, as was a nun into whose vagina a snake entered when she was meditating in the lotus posture.[77] To reduce the possibility of being sexually assaulted, nuns were required to live together and always travel in groups.

Even in numbers the nuns got into trouble. Once a group of nuns spotted a huge penis, perhaps that of an animal, lying in the road. The villagers noticed the nuns gawking at the giant sex organ and complained to Buddha about his disciples' behavior. Down came the word, "No more unseemly staring at a penis, animal or human."[78]

A number of courtesans joined the Order of Nuns. One such nun composed this bittersweet verse on growing old:

> Black was my hair, the color of honeybees, curled at the
>   ends—
> Now just like rough hemp.

Fragrant was my hair, full of perfumed flowers—
Now it smells like dog fur.

Thick as a grove, nicely combed and ornamented—
Now I am nearly bald.

My eyebrows looked as if they had been painted by a master
artist—
Now they can hardly be seen.

As brilliant as flashing jewels, deep and black were my
eyes—
Now they are dull and dim.

Long, beautiful, and delicate was my nose—
Now a pendulous bump.

Perfectly shaped were my ear lobes—
Now, all wrinkled and droopy.

My teeth were as lovely as white flowers—
Now they are cracked and yellow.

My voice was as sweet as a nightingale's—
Now it is thin and broken.

Beautiful was my throat, like a polished conch shell—
Now it sags with folds.

My arms were once round and smooth—
Now they are weak and shriveled.

Lovely were my hands, adorned with diamonds—
Now knotted and twisted roots.

Full and round were my breasts, close-set, delectable, and
lofty—
Now empty water bags.

My luscious body was like a tablet of gold—
Now it is nothing but stringy lumps.

My thighs were as strong and firm as an elephant's trunk—
Now they are as brittle bamboo.

My legs were shapely, adorned with gold anklets—
Now, just sticks.

As soft as down were my feet—
Now two ugly pieces of flesh.

Worn out and decrepit now, an old house with its plaster
    falling off—
Just like Buddha said it would be! [79]

The puritan elders have three main defenses against attraction to
the opposite sex. The first is, "Think of every female (male) that
you encounter as either your mother, sister, or daughter (father,
brother, son)." [80] In fact, if one accepts the theory of endless transmigration as literal truth, every other human being has been, at one
time or another, such a relative.

The second defense is recollection of the loathsomeness of the
body, described in detail above, and the third is "watchfulness," as
summarized in this famous dialogue between Buddha and Ānanda.
(If you are female, substitute "men" for "women.")

> "Lord, how should we behave toward women?"
> "Not look at them."
> "But what if we must look at them?"
> "Not speak to them."
> "But what if we must speak to them?"
> "Keep wide awake." [81]

In this regard, the elder Mahā-Tissa was the ideal monk. Once he
was walking along a road contemplating the transiency of life. An
attractive woman, lovely as a goddess, passed by and smiled at him.
A little later the woman's husband—the couple had quarreled and
he was pursuing her—came up to the elder and asked him, "Did
you see a woman go by?" Mahā-Tissa replied, "A bag of bones
walked past me, but I cannot tell you if it was a man or a woman." [82]

Watchfulness is still the rule in the puritan Buddhist tradition.
When a monk addresses a group of laypeople in Burma, for example, he is hidden behind a screen to prevent him from being captivated by anyone in his audience or vice versa. [83]

In Buddha's time, as today, there were those who conceded the
necessity of strict rules and guidelines for men and women not in
full control of their faculties—"just as rain ruins an ill-thatched hut,
passion destroys an ill-trained mind." [84] But what about arhats,
saints who have attained awakening and comprehended the Bud-

dhist teaching? Since Buddha has acknowledged that their minds
are purified, why should they not savor the joys of love and gratification of the senses?

Buddha's ambiguous reply was "Sexual passion can no more
cling to an arhat than water to a lotus leaf." [85]

The puritan elders, male and female, took this to mean that if one
controls sex at its origin, the genitalia cease to function and celibacy
is the natural outcome. According to this view, an arhat is a kind of
third sex; indeed, in some Buddhist costumes it is often difficult to
distinguish the wearer's gender. Asexuality is one of the ramifica-
tions of arhathood—on that level one has no further interest in sex
and hence no desire to have intercourse. And not only intercourse.
A real arhat is also supposed to be free of the desire to be touched
by, talk with, look at, dream about, or long to meet in paradise a
member of the opposite sex; nor can an arhat be a voyeur. [86] A number of laymen and laywomen are shown to have achieved arhathood, but then they are characterized as immediately taking vows
of celibacy and entering the Order as soon as circumstances permitted. In short, enlightenment and sexual activity are incompatible—
such was the view of the puritan elders, a faction with proponents
in nearly every Buddhist tradition.

Sex can be, undeniably, the source of much terrible suffering and
mental distress, and if not properly managed, it can be absolute poi-
son. Celibacy can be a powerful antidote to sexual afflictions. More
positively, when one is free of family ties and other physical and
emotional bonds, it is far easier to work unimpeded for the welfare
of all beings, the raison d'être of Buddhism. This is the rationale
behind the celibacy expected of the Dalai Lama and other high Tibetan lamas, for example, who are taken from their families at an
early age and raised in a sexually neutral environment. The children
are not cuddled or kissed; they must not develop physical and emotional dependence on any individual, nor become the exclusive
focus of such attention. As incarnate Buddhas, the lamas are supposed to embrace every sentient being in a non-sexual way. [87] Once
sex is totally removed from the equation one may deal with others
on a higher plane, without recourse to sexual posturing. Understood in this manner, celibacy is a valid, indeed essential option for
certain Buddhists. [88]

In reality, though, few can reside in a state of true celibacy in both body *and* mind. Ānanda, for instance, was Buddha's personal attendant for years. He became Buddha's follower primarily because of the Master's transcendence of sex: "When anyone becomes inflamed by sexual passion, his mind becomes disturbed and confused, he loses self-control, and he becomes reckless and crude. Besides, in sexual intercourse the blood becomes inflamed and adulterated with impure secretions. Naturally, from such a source there can never originate an aureole of such transcendently pure and golden brightnesss as I have seen emanating from the person of [Buddha, . . . and that is why I became] one of his true followers." [89]

With that kind of example ever before him, we might expect Ānanda to be the ideal celibate, but no—it was very rough going even for him. Ānanda seems to have had a much more pleasant personality than many of the other lugubrious monks and was consequently a great favorite of the women in the community. It was Ānanda who lobbied the Buddha for the establishment of the Order of Nuns. Women, including nuns, continually fell in love with Ānanda (his name means "Beloved") and more than once he had to be rescued by miraculous intervention from the clutches of some adoring female. [90] He did, however, stay the course, and he remains an inspiration for celibate Buddhists. [91]

While celibacy may be a boon for some, it is a bane for others. If the incidents appearing in the *Vinaya* are any indication of the problem, it is clear that many of the monks and nuns were tormented by sex despite the elaborate safety net devised by Buddha to assist them. (Not long after the Order was established, one monk chopped off his sex organs in an attempt to rid himself of the problem once and for all; Buddha rejected that solution, and self-castration was expressly prohibited.) [92] One nun of Buddha's time complained that even after twenty-five years in the Order, "every thought was soaked with desire." [93] Two thousand years later we have the same lament. When asked what was the most difficult part of being a monk, seventeen out of twenty Asian monks replied, "Resisting sexual temptation." [94] There is an "in-house" joke among westerners who have taken Buddhist monastic ordination that "no one leaves the order because they cannot take food after midday." In other words, total abstention from sex is by far the most difficult precept to keep. [95]

Since so few renunciates were able to keep their vows, Buddhist monks and nuns throughout the East have always been caricatured as the most sex-crazed of human beings, not to be trusted under any circumstance. Every country in the East has a collection of ribald tales cataloguing the iniquities of Buddhist monks and nuns.[96] Here are samples of some of the less scandalous stories.

After years of living in a monastery, a monk was taken to the city and treated to a night in a brothel. The next morning he exclaimed to himself, "The people here are most peculiar. From the front they are just like the nuns and from the back just like the acolytes."[97]

A monk accompanied by his novice visited a nun. The monk sent the novice out to buy some rice wine. As soon as the novice left, the monk and nun threw off their robes and embraced each other. Immediately overcome with passion, the pair cried out, "I'm dying! I'm dying," a phrase often uttered by people in the Far East when they are in the throes of orgasm. After the couple completed their lovemaking they were surprised to find the novice still standing outside the door. "Why didn't you buy the wine?" the monk asked. The novice replied, "If you both die, who is going to pay for it?"[98]

It often appears that the only ones who are not troubled by sex are older men well past their prime. In fact, impotent middle-aged men in south Asian countries sometimes join the Order to escape the sexual demands of their wives.[99] Others have gotten sex out of their systems before entering the Order; in some communities it is not unusual for a quarter of the monks to have been married previously.[100] And even the oldest abbots are not immune to feminine charms. In Thailand, if a family has a special request to make of a temple, they always delegate their prettiest members to make the supplication, because abbots find it hard to turn down young girls.

Since so many puritan elders were unable to come to grips with their sexuality, an extremely unfortunate tendency developed: women began to be blamed as the origin of all sexual perversion— just by being female. Even though the statement "Every man has been at one time a woman, and every woman at one time a man"[101] is found in some texts, an appalling proportion of Buddhist literature in all traditions is devoted to vilifying women as depravity incarnate—insatiable, vile, degraded, and nothing but woe. In this view, women are accused of never tiring of three things: "sexual intercourse, adornment, and childbearing."[102] Buddhist texts are relentlessly masculine in orientation, and women are frequently condemned as being utterly incapable of attaining enlightenment.[103] The best thing about paradise, some Buddhists believed, was that there are no women there.[104]

Modern-day feminists have indignantly catalogued the offending texts and rightly denounced such attitudes.[105] I will cite only one typical example from that distressing literature:

A mother(!) wished to instil in her son understanding of the wickedness of women. She told him to visit his teacher once more and request instruction in the *Book of Sorrow*. The teacher agreed, under the following conditions: "You must care for my mother, who is now one hundred and twenty years old. Bathe her gently every day, telling her things like, 'You are still so beautiful—when you were younger you must have been divine,' and 'How I love to touch your body.' Report to me everything she says."

The lad followed his teacher's instructions, and the old hag foolishly believed that the boy was in love with her. "Do you desire me?" she asked him.

"Yes, very much," he lied.

"Take me."

"My teacher—your son—would not allow such a thing."

"Kill him!"

"What are you saying?! He is my teacher!"

"Then I will kill him myself!"

The teacher was informed of the plot, and he and the boy carved a wooden replica of a man. The blind old woman was taken by the boy to the statue and without an instant's hesitation plunged an axe into it. When her evil intentions were exposed, she shrieked and dropped dead on the spot.

The boy returned home and was asked by his mother, "What did you learn from the *Book of Sorrow?*"

> Full of unbridled lust, an all-devouring fire
> Are women, frantic in their passion.
> I will forsake sex forever
> And live peacefully in a hermitage.[106]

This warped view of women is the product of unstable minds incapable of coping with sex; fortunately, there were others who interpreted Buddhism in a more balanced fashion.

3

The Jewel in the Lotus: Buddhist Tantra

While there has always been in Buddhism a pronounced puritan element that was virulently antisex and pro-monastic, it was clear to a number of other Buddhists that celibacy in itself was no great virtue. As we saw in the previous chapter, many monks and nuns remained obsessed with sex despite the safety net of strict rules and regulations, and frequently many members of the Order of Celibates ended up further from their professed goal of passionlessness that when they began. Furthermore, a one-sided emphasis on withdrawal from daily life and total shunning of the opposite sex was untenable for the vast majority of Buddhists who had to function in the world to, among other things, provide the wherewithal for the survival of the Order of Celibates. Although it was generally acknowledged to be more difficult, enlightened living had to be possible within the context of ordinary existence (which, of course, includes the sexual dimension)—otherwise Buddhism would have had very limited appeal.

Others maintained that Buddha's message had nothing to do with celibacy—insight and compassion were the two pillars of Buddhism, and those two faculties could be developed regardless of one's station in life. Such is the position presented in the *Vimalakīrti Nirdeśa Sūtra,*[1] featuring an astute layman who confounds all Buddha's monastic disciples.

In this sutra, indeed, the tension that perennially exists between monastic and lay practitioners is depicted in the sharpest focus. Since a layman is the hero in this story, the monks are portrayed as dullards. They are completely befuddled by the wise Vimalakīrti, who was, we are told, supremely skilled in techniques that lead to the liberation of all beings, not of just a few select celibates. Vimalakīrti had a wife, children, and a host of female attendants, yet he remained untainted by desire. He freely mixed with all manner of people—on occasion, Vimalakīrti could be found in a brothel or a wine shop—all the time pointing the way to salvation. The monks were no match for him.[2]

Sāriputra, the wisest of Buddha's disciples, was sitting in solitary meditation beneath a tree deep in the forest when he was suddenly approached by Vimalakīrti. The layman told the monk in no uncertain terms, "This is not the way to meditate. You must place yourself in a state of contemplation where there is neither body nor mind; where you manifest ordinary behavior while in nirvana; where you act like a normal person without losing your spiritual nature; where your mind neither settles nor moves about; and where nothing troubles you at any stage of practice. In short, you must attain liberation without avoiding the passions that rule the world!" Sāriputra was dumbstruck.[3]

Subhūti, another monastic disciple, had a similar harrowing run-in with Vimalakīrti. One day while on his mendicant rounds, Subhūti appeared at Vimalakīrti's door. The layman offered Subhūti some tasty morsels, for which his household was famed, but first admonished him, "Unless you defame the Buddha, ignore his teachings, and keep company with demons, you are not worthy of this food." Just as Subhūti was about to flee in horror, Vimalakīrti cried out, "Wait! Do not be afraid. All things are mere phantoms—words, too. Do not be confused by them. Understand the true nature of all things, and you will be liberated."[4]

Later in the sutra there is a delightful exchange between Sāriputra, spokesman for the monks, and a little girl. A shower of flowers pours down on the assembly gathered in Vimalakīrti's room, and Sāriputra is aghast that the blossoms stick only to the monks and not to the richly dressed Bodhisattvas. When he asks for an explanation, the little girl volunteers, "You monks are full of discriminative thoughts, dislikes, and other fears, so the flowers of attachment naturally cling to you."

The dialogue continues, with the little girl gradually revealing how attached Sāriputra is to his monastic non-attachment. Such false pride is dangerous, she warns him, but then he asks in a supercilious tone, "If you are so wise, why are you still a woman?" (As noted in the previous chapter it was—and still is in some quarters—believed that enlightenment cannot be attained in a female state.) Thereupon the little girl gleefully employs her magic powers to transform Sāriputra into a female with her form and then asks him, with much glee, "Well, how do you like being a girl?" She further chides him, "In reality, there is neither male nor female."[5]

Later on in this sutra, Mañjuśrī, the Bodhisattva of Wisdom, states unequivocally, "Without entering the ocean of desire it is impossible to obtain an illumined mind."[6] We are also told of women who intentionally become courtesans in order to win men over; having caught them with the hook of desire, such female Bodhisattvas can teach those men to manifest the Buddha-mind.

The female counterpart of Vimalakīrti is Queen Śrīmālā, heroine of the sutra *The Lion's Roar of Queen Śrīmālā*.[7] Like Vimalakīrti, she is portrayed as a contemporary of Buddha. As mentioned previously, it was an article of faith for many puritan Buddhists that females were incapable of attaining the higher levels of realization because of their intrinsically inferior nature. *The Lion's Roar of Queen Śrīmālā* demolishes that view, placing female lay bodhisattvas on equal footing with lay and monastic males. Women, the sutra makes clear, are just as able as men to practice and teach the higher truths.

In the sūtra there is an interesting passage that alludes to the breaking up of the Buddhist community because of disagreements between monastic and lay practitioners. The sūtra also alludes to the forming of a group of lay bodhisattvas who maintain the Teaching after their own fashion, independent of the Order of Celibates.[8]

Later on in the text, arhats are criticized for becoming monks primarily out of fear, for attempting to circumvent samsara by totally negative, one-sided means. "Nirvana," the sutra states, "consists of the elimination of all faults and impurites," a condition not dependent on either the lay or monastic state; if one realizes the innate purity of mind, there will be liberation.[9]

Even though she was a queen, Śrīmālā was unattached to material things, ever aware of the nature of reality, and a good friend to all those in distress. Buddha praised her profound understanding as "most excellent," more valuable than the worship of a hundred thousand enlightened beings.

There are three other remarkable but little-known sutras that strongly champion the cause of female Buddhahood. In the text called *Chapters on Skillful Means*[10] the monastic philosopher Subhūti is put to the test by an enchanting young lady decorated with gold and purple and as lovely as a lotus flower. Subhūti calls at the lady's house to receive almsfood. "What!" the lady chides him. "Are you as a renunciate still attached to food?"

"Yes," Subhūti replies, "I must eat to assuage my hunger."

"If you are enlightened," she says, "and have mastered the doctrine of emptiness, surely you shouldn't be bothered by something as trival as hunger!"

The dialogue continues in this fashion, and the lady has Subhūti on the defensive the whole time. Finally she concludes, "You must live free from all attachment and leave no trace wherever you happen to be."

Impressed with lady's acumen, Subhūti asks, "Who are you? Where are you from?"

She tells him, "I am an emanation from the Buddha-nature, originating in emptiness, yet manifest in the body of a woman."

"Are you married?" Subhūti wants to know.

"I have many, many husbands," she says. "If a man enjoys sensual pleasures, I give him all he desires and then enlighten him to Buddhism through passion."

"Isn't that immoral?" Subhūti questions.

"What I do is no different from what you do. When you request alms and provisions, a generous patron gives them to you so that you can practice Buddhism. When a man needs something from me I give him the object of his desires while awakening his Buddha-mind."

She goes on to state that women better understand the nature of sex, and that is why she is manifest as a female. Suddenly, however, she transforms herself into a twelve-year-old boy, showing that Buddha-nature has nothing to do with gender. The boy later changes back into a woman even more stunning than before.

Subhūti reports back to Buddha. The Master informs Subhūti

that the lady is really a very great bodhisattva, one who enlightens sentient beings by employing "the skillful means of pleasure." Just then the lady, with a retinue of five hundred female attendants, appears before them. Subhūti prostrates himself before the lady as a gesture of respect. Shocked, Sāriputra shoots at Subhūti, "What are you doing? Only non-Buddhists bow to women!"

"Who are you to judge who is a Buddhist and who is not?" Subhūti shoots back in reply.

More than a little vexed, Sāriputra demands to know, "How do you tell a true Buddhist?"

The lady herself answers: "A Buddhist follows Buddha's teachings and is compassionate toward Buddhist and non-Buddhist alike. A Buddhist can be a woman, adorned with jewels and wearing fine clothes, beautiful and fragrant, who embraces all sentient beings and grants all their desires. Her Buddha-mind remains intact under all conditions, and therefore she is superior to monks and arhats who cling to a one-sided attachment to meditation and asceticism."

Inexplicably, the sutra ends on a very strange and sour note. Despite her eloquent defense of female Buddhahood, the lady suddenly pleads with Buddha to change her and her retinue into males. Buddha does so on the spot, and male chauvinism seems to prevail once again.

The *Ocean Dragon King Sutra* has a happier ending.[11] In this text, a girl called Ratnavatī remonstrates to Mahākāśyapa, another of Buddha's top monastic disciples, that women desire supreme enlightenment just as strongly as men do. Mahākāśyapa tells her, "You cannot attain enlightenment, because you are a woman."

Ratnavatī counters, "If one is pure in body and mind, and if one's heart is set on attaining enlightenment, Buddhahood is within one's grasp. If a woman cannot attain the highest enlightenment, neither can a man. Enlightenment has nothing to do with male or female."

Mahākāśyapa concedes, "If you put it like that you must be right," and Buddha predicts Ratnavatī's eventual attainment of supreme enlightenment without adding any stipulations about male transformation.

Most remarkable of all is the *Splendid Dharma Gate Sutra*.[12] Here, the heroine is a radiant courtesan named, intriguingly, the Golden

54

One of Illustrious Virtue. She and Mañjuśrī engage in a long dialogue regarding the innate purity of the senses, the identity of passion and enlightenment, and the ultimate unreality of all external characteristics. The Golden One champions the necessity of male and female union as the root of all existence. "Without sexual union, there would be no one born capable of experiencing the great bliss of enlightenment." She instructs Buddha's disciples not to get entangled by passion but also not to abandon it either. A state of equilibrium between the polarities of passion and the void is the ideal. Even as she makes sweet love to them, the Golden One instructs her patrons in the intricacies of Buddhism.

Still another important sutra that downplays the distinction between lay and monastic Buddhists is *The Pilgrimage of Sudhana*.[13] In this text, the young seeker Sudhana sets out to attain supreme awakening and along the way encounters fifty-three spiritual guides. The striking thing about these guides is the diversity of their backgrounds—in addition to the expected Buddhist monks, nuns, and bodhisattvas, the guides include non-Buddhist sages, gods and goddesses, kings, beggars, scholars, tradesmen, hermits, perfumers, old men and women, young boys and girls, and even a ship's captain. All these spiritual guides have something unique to impart to Sudhana.

On his pilgrimage Sudhana comes face to face with three ravishing beauties, who teach him much. The first is Prabhūtā,[14] a lay devotee of Buddha, "young, slim, fresh, in the blossom of youth, radiantly beautiful, her hair hanging down." Although she resides in a splendid palace, Prabhūtā dresses simply in a white robe and no adornments. Prabhūtā's duty, she informs Sudhana, is to provide sentient beings with the nourishment of enlightenment. The vessel is always full and can satisfy any hunger.

Later, Sudhana is sent to meet Acalā,[15] a woman of "inconceivable physical majesty. The radiance of her complexion, the proportion of her body, her fragrance, and the magnificence of her aura were unexcelled." One night Acalā tells Sudhana, "I had a vision of Buddha and joined with him in spiritual union." Thereafter, she became the purest of women—like the Virgin Mary, a being untainted by lust both from within and without. Gazing on her form, men were immediately purged of their base desires. We must, she instructs Sudhana, develop the mind of sharing, providing each sentient being with the means with which to attain liberation.

On the other hand, the third beauty of Sudhana, Vasumitrā,[16] had a much different role to play. A worshiper of Agni, the God of Fire, Vasumitrā had golden skin, black hair, and a well-proportioned body decorated with countless jeweled ornaments. Her practice was to appear to men in the most pleasing form they could imagine and then transmute their intense passion into spiritual bliss. Some men could be transformed just by seeing Vasumitrā, but others needed to hold, kiss, or embrace her fully. Vasumitrā likened her practice to "a womb that receives all sentient beings without rejection"; she used passion to lead men to the "ultimately dispassionate," urging them to enter her in order to go beyond physical. Vasumitrā instructed Sudhana in the skill of achieving dispassion by using all the senses. (Significantly, Sudhana was sent to Vasumitrā by the nun Simhavijṛmbhitā, a master of seeing through all vain imaginings, to learn how to actually implement the teachings by applying one's insight practically.)

Other texts tell of bodhisattvas who abandon vows of celibacy they have scrupulously observed for several billion years to bring a female disciple closer to enlightenment. Indeed, one text openly declares, "If a woman falls violently in love with a bodhisattva and is about to sacrifice her life for him, it is his duty to save her life by satisfying all her desires."[17] Here are several typical stories in that vein.

In Māra's entourage there were two hundred divine maidens who once cried out with desire, "If any man would dally and make love to us we would follow him anywhere." A sharp-eared bodhisattva heard about this, transformed himself into two hundred gods of perfection, and satisfied all the maidens simultaneously. Now happily fulfilled, they paid him great honor; the bodhisattva expounded the Dharma to them in the appropriate manner, and the maidens raised their minds toward enlightenment.[18]

The legend of the Bodhisattva of Linked Bones was very popular in China: a foreign-looking beauty one day appeared in a village. The exquisite girl made tender love to anyone who sought her favors, and no man who shared her bed was ever the same again.

After her death, at age twenty-four, an eminent monk from central Asia appeared before her grave and held a special funeral service. When asked the reason for such reverence, the monk told the villagers, "That girl was, in reality, the Bodhisattva of Linked Bones, committed to granting whatever was requested of her in order to lead man to salvation." The girl's tomb was opened, revealing a skeleton of bones delicately linked together.[19]

In Japan, the bodhisattvas Fugen (Samantabhadra) and Kannon (Avalokiteśvara) were popularly thought to incarnate themselves as beautiful women. For years a virtuous priest practiced asceticism, longing for a glimpse of Fugen. One night in a dream he was told to visit the abode of a famous courtesan. When the priest entered her room, he saw the girl in the center entertaining a host of young men. Then all at once she was transformed into Fugen, radiant and majestic, and the little ditty she had been singing to her customers became words from the Buddhist sutras. The priest noticed that only he could see her. Later, Fugen appeared to him and said, "Tell no one what you have seen. It is only those with uncorrupt hearts that can behold me in my true form."[20]

Another story about Fugen was made into a well-known Noh drama. The wandering poet-monk Saigyō one night requested lodging at a certain residence. The mistress of the home refused because she was alone. Saigyō passed to her this poetic plea:

Before I renounced the world
Your rejection would have been just,
But now why should you
Deny this black-robed monk
A night's lodging in this dream world?

The lady was adamant:

I know that you are
One who has renounced the world,
But in this dream world
I must spare you even
The thought of attachment.

In the Noh drama the lady later appears to Saigyō as Fugen, and she tells him that her rejection was really an act of kindness designed to protect his reputation.[21]

Kannon, the Goddess of Compassion, often appears in both Chinese and Japanese art as "The Maiden with a Fish Basket." A charming young girl appeared in the village market one day, and all the eligible men there sought her hand in marriage. The girl told them, "I will wed the man who can memorize the *Kannon Sutra* in one night." Since there were twenty successful candidates the next morning, she said, "No, I will wed the one who can memorize the *Diamond Sutra* in one night." Ten passed that test. "Still too many," she said. "I will wed the man who can memorize the *Lotus Sutra* in three days." One determined young man accomplished that impressive feat, and the pair planned to wed. Just prior to the ceremony the girl took ill and withered away, and the groom had to be content with her memory. Sometime later a holy monk came along and had the girl's tomb opened. It contained a body of solid gold.[22]

(In Japan, pleasure girls not infrequently took as their professional name "Little Goddess of Compassion." Even today, some Japanese men employ the euphemism "going to worship Kannon" when they plan to visit a striptease show.)

Although Vimalakīrti, Srīmālā, the female Bodhisattvas, Sudhana, and all the rest are mythical, similar figures certainly existed. Here are a few documented examples from the early days of Buddhism (more case histories will be given later in the sections on Tantra and Zen).

Kumārajīva, who was born in central Asia in the fourth century C.E., entered the Buddhist order at age seven. An extremely brilliant student, Kumārajīva became a master of exoteric and esoteric Buddhism. The monk was summoned by the emperor to China to teach Buddhist doctrine and supervise the translation of texts, but on the way he was kidnapped by a local lord who wanted to keep the famous scholar in his own domain. Following a stalemate that lasted nearly twenty years, the emperor finally dispatched an army to subdue the lord and bring Kumārajīva to the capital.

The emperor, a man of practical Chinese bent, wanted Kumārajīva's vast talents to be somehow preserved. Hoping that some of the monk's brilliance would rub off on his heirs, the emperor presented Kumārajīva with ten young brides, commanding him to father as many children as possible. Kumārajīva felt obliged to comply, and his transgression against his monastic precepts did nothing to diminish his reputation as one of the patriarchs of Chinese Buddhism and as among the great Buddhist scholars/translators of all time. (None of his offspring, alas, come anywhere near matching his intellect.) [23]

Won Hyo, nicknamed the "Unbridled Monk," was a Korean master of the seventh century. He is venerated as that country's most profound and creative thinker. One day, one of Won Hyo's masters took him to a brothel. "It is not good for a monk to live in heaven all the time," the master said to Won Hyo. "It is necessary to visit hell once in a while to assist the inmates there, too." After spending the night with the prettiest girl in the house, Won Hyo cast off his robes and danced through the streets, singing, "The universe is just like this!" Won Hyo had the characters "no obstacle" embroidered on the crotch of his trousers and entertained any lady who desired his company. He later became the lover of Princess Kwa, and she bore his child. Won Hyo's motto was, "Only one with no worries and no fears can conquer life, death, and transmigration" (a verse from the *Avataṃsaka Sūtra* of which *The Pilgrimage of Sudhana* forms a part). [24]

Although he may not have deserved the reputation, Won Hyo's contemporary, K'uei-chi, the First Chinese Patriarch of the Mind Only School, was celebrated for traveling with three big carts—one for his sutras, one for meat and wine, and one for women. [25]

The historical figure of Khemā of Great Wisdom may be the prototype of both Queen Śrīmālā and Prajñāpāramitā, the female Bodhisattva of Transcendental Wisdom. Decked out in all her regal splendor, Khemā grasped Buddha's teaching the first time she met him, and attained awakening on the spot, still clad in her glorious garments, decorated with jewels, and redolent of perfume. Later she became a nun, but her initial realization was obtained while she was a laywoman of surpassing beauty and charm. [26]

Then there is the example of Ambapāli, the greatest courtesan of the day. When Buddha saw her for the first time he is said to have exclaimed, "With all her beauty, which enslaves even kings and princes, she also possesses great calm and steadfastness. Women of such character are in truth rare in this world!"[27]

There was also the example of Visākhā the Benefactress, a beauty who bathed herself in vats of perfumed water and adorned herself in the finest garments while devoting herself to Buddha's cause. She was said to have given birth to ten sons and ten daughters; she lived to be 120 years old but always retained the appearance and spirit of a sixteen-year-old. The Buddha continually praised her great charity and held her up as the ideal Buddhist laywoman—beautiful, generous, kind and faithful.[28]

An emphasis on the essential equality of lay and monastic Buddhism; acceptance, or at least tolerance of the sexual dimension of life; and the validity of using sex, if the need arises, as a form of skillful means characterize the attitude of the moderate Mahāyāna Buddhists. More extreme are the Tantric Buddhists, those who see sex as the most powerful aid in the quest for liberation.[29]

Literal-minded scholars have attempted, fruitlessly, to trace the origin of Tantra, hoping to pin down its beginnings in some particular time and place, but they fail to realize that Tantric perceptions are an integral, albeit frequently suppressed part of human psychology. Many sages, East and West, have recognized that "Detachment can only come after attachment" and that "By passion the world is bound and by passion it is released."[30]

Tantra, in whatever guise, bases itself on these principles: the affirmation of life in all its forms and the validity of the phenomenal world; the innate purity of natural conditions; the complexity of the psychophysical makeup of human beings; the body as a microcosm of the universe; and the necessity of realizing the truth in this present mode of existence. One of the prime components of existence is sex, a vibrant force that vivifies the human entity from conception. Ruthless suppression of the natural propensity to seek union with a member of the opposite sex sours people, followers of the Tantra believe, making them morbid, compulsive, and neurotic. Annihilation of the sexual impulse is impossible for all but the very few, so it is far better for us to redirect and transform our natural desires. The undeniable bliss one feels during sexual climax

Tantric Buddha and his consort at the center of the universe (detail). Followers of the Vajrayana, the Tantric Vehicle of Buddhism, maintained that the complete teaching could only be realized when cosmic emptiness was united with terrestrial wisdom. Here a naked Buddha embraces his female counterpart; joined at the heart, mystic syllables radiate from their union, creating the forces which sustain the universe.

can be, if understood properly, a religious experience of the highest order—indeed, sexual intercourse became the Tantric symbol supreme for the Great Bliss of Liberation.

Tantric Buddhists, advocates of the Vajrayāna, were dissatisfied with the unhealthy emphasis on celibacy and withdrawal maintained by the puritan elders, and they were impatient with the grand philosophizing and convoluted intellectual superstructure of much of the Mahāyāna; they wanted instead something more positive, direct, and concrete. Sex should be part of the Buddhist equation, some insisted: "Sex was the main preoccupation of Gotama when he was a prince in the palace, which must have had something to do with his subsequent Buddhahood, so why shouldn't we follow in his footsteps?"

From the beginning in Buddhism it was implicit that "nirvana is samsara; the passions themselves constitute enlightenment." Prior to Gotama's Supreme Awakening, the world appeared to him to be samsara—hopelessly confused, corrupt, and evil. When he became a Buddha, however, everything was perceived in the radiance of nirvana, and existence, for him, turned orderly, wholesome, and good. The external factors surrounding Gotama/Buddha had not changed, of course; it was his consciousness that had been transformed. In other words, samsara is a disease of the mind, not a fixed condition. When the mind is overrun by uncontrollable thoughts and fears and clouded by passion, the world can seem a dreadful place; when the mind is free of all blemishes, calm and bright, there is nothing but nirvana.

This is the point of the story of Vaśistha, a brahmin who had practiced austerities for six thousand years of incarnations without result—he was no closer to liberation than when he started. A seer directed him to a magic kingdom (located in China in some accounts). There Vaśistha was shocked to discover Buddha flushed with wine and dallying with a host of gorgeous women. The outraged Vaśistha accused Buddha of immoral behavior. Buddha calmly explained the true nature of the Tantric Diamond Path: "Liberation from all limiting conditions." Vaśistha was convinced, and finally attained enlightenment through "unrestrained application of Tantric principles." [31] Similarly, Saraha, one of the patriarchs of Tantric Buddhism, declared, "It was only after I slept with a woman that I became a pure monk." [32]

Passions, Tantric Buddhists state, are the raw material of enlightenment—not obstacles, but true building blocks. Sex, the greatest of passions, could if used properly be our greatest ally instead of our deadliest foe. In the Tantra, the sex act is neutral; if one acts like an animal or is in any way evil-minded, the repercussions are most grave, but if one behaves as a bodhisattva, liberation is close at hand for both partners. Sexual intercourse is generally marred by animal appetite and superficial relief. Even here, though, one or both of the participants usually has a fleeting experience of

Buddhist lovers. Although marriage never had the status of a sacrament in Buddhism, the art of love as a spiritual practice always had many adherents in various Buddhist sects.

non-dual bliss. Followers of the Tantra, in a state of acute arousal, aspire to make that experience permanent and of cosmic significance. For Vajrayāna Buddhists, such communion idealizes the emptiness and supreme bliss of awakening.

The sexual union represents the highest bliss. The female element is an embodiment of *prajñā*, transcendental wisdom; the woman's *yoni* is the abode of pure bliss. The male element symbolizes *upāya*, the skillful means needed to actualize enlightenment; the man's *liṅgam* is the diamond hardness of Buddhist emptiness. The mother-father (*yab-yum*) images of the Tibetan Buddhists reproduce the Vajrayāna vision three-dimensionally—the polar opposites of the phenomenal world in perfect communion, at ease, balanced, and fulfilled. Such dynamic sexual images are thought to depict the dignity of the phenomenal world, not is degradation, as is believed in both puritan Buddhism and Christianity. The Tibetan mantra *oṃ maṇi padme hūṃ* is a condensed form of the same teaching: *oṃ* = the origin of all life; *maṇi* = the jewel of the male principle; *padme* = the lotus of the female polarity; *hūṃ* = the union of the two in undifferentiated consciousness, and the reintegration of emptiness with form, wisdom with skillful means, nirvana with samsara: "From that union a pure knowledge arises, which explains the nature of all things."

A guidebook to Shambhala—Shangri-la—describes a seeker's initiation in Tantric Buddhist sex:

> The fabulous maidens who dwell [in the land just before Shambhala] have lovely moon faces, beautiful as lotus blossoms, with eyes like blue flowers. Sashes of fine cloth decorated with pearls adorn their golden bodies. Their graceful, jeweled limbs move like tree branches swaying in a gentle breeze.
>
> As soon as the maidens see you, they will go wild with passion and swarm around like excited bees craving honey. Smiling and looking at you out of the corners of their eyes so that it feels as if your minds merge in one, they will embrace you and wrap their seductive limbs around your body like vines around a tree. Why not take pleasure with these maidens who have attained the purity and spiritual power of enlightened beings? Taste the honey of their breasts, extended toward you like flowers offering you their nectar.
>
> As you do, a great surge of joy and bliss will carry you soaring beyond all bodily sensation. The heat of an inner fire, like the fire that blazes on the southern edge of the universe, will rise through your body, burning away the thickets of mental obscurations [and] it will purify your body and transform it into the indestructible diamond body of bliss. In what other way can you so quickly attain it?[33]

A number of Vajrayāna texts have come down to us that describe Tantric Buddhist practices. The compilation of these texts must have been very haphazard, for they are, in general, a bewildering jumble of the sublime, the horrid, and the ridiculous. Most contain an explicit warning: "These teachings will, if correctly understood, allow one to attain Buddhahood in this very life; if misconstrued, however, one will burn in hell forever." Few are truly qualified for these practices, and genuine Tantric masters were extremely selective of their students. Buddhist gurus typically insisted that prospective candidates complete years of Hīnayāna (monastic) and Mahāyāna (moral) training before initiation. Some teachers were so cautious that they maintained that the rites should only be visualized and not actually carried out. In any case, the sole motivation of a Tantric Buddhist must be the wish to liberate all sentient beings from suffering and distress.

Sex, naturally, is a central concern of the Vajrayāna texts. Some, in fact, begin with the sentence, "Thus I have heard: When the Buddha was reposing in the vagina of his consort he delivered this discourse. . . ."[34] The Buddhist tantras were organized into four levels of difficulty—*kriyā-*, *caryā-*, *yoga-*, and *annuttara-yoga*—corresponding to the stages of sexual love: smiles, longing gazes, embrace, and union.

In dramatic contrast to the misogynist sentiments so often found in Hīnayāna and Mahāyāna texts, women are worshiped unconditionally in the Buddhist tantras—one text declares openly, "Buddhahood resides in the female sex organs"[35]—and are venerated as vehicles of *mahāmudrā,* the Great Symbol of Enlightenment. A Lady of Supreme Liberation is described in one tantra as "Neither too tall nor too short, neither quite black nor quite white, but dark like a lotus leaf. Her breath is sweet, her perspiration has the scent of musk, and her yoni is as fragrant as lotus blossoms and aloe wood. She is calm, resolute, and pleasant in speech, with lustrous hair and a luscious body—altogether delightful!"[36]

This Tantric rite is detailed in the same Vajrayāna text:

The male participant should visualize himself as Lord Buddha, and the female participant should imagine herself as the Lady of Transcendental Wisdom. They should first sit facing each other and gaze upon their partner with intense desire. They kiss and embrace tenderly, and she then has him suck her lotus (*yoni*). Next she demands the ultimate from him, asking if he is capable of eating her feces and drinking her urine.

"Look at my beautiful lotus," she instructs him, "decorated in the middle with a stamen. Place your feet on my shoulders and make your *vajra* stalk enter my lotus."

"Give me," she cries out, inflamed with passion, "a thousand, one hundred thousand, ten million, one hundred million strokes!"

The man is counseled at this stage to remain still while the woman provides the motion, so he can keep his mind concentrated on the extreme pleasure. Following this initial meditative union, the pair is enjoined to engage in the following love postures: pleasure-evoking, swing-rocking, knee-holding, thigh-rubbing, foot-moving, ground-pressing, equal-summit, variegated, honeycomb, mounted on the machine, one leg up, tortoise, and "every way auspicious." (Although brief descriptions are given, the exact performance of each posture is unclear—firsthand instruction seems necessary.)

To complete the rite, the Lord is to kiss and worship every part of the Lady's body. Following this demanding workout, the couple is advised to restore themselves with fish, meat, and wine. The Tantra draws this conclusion: "Every time a couple make love, if they view each other as Lord and Lady, when the stalk enters the lotus there will surely be enlightenment."

It seems that the participants in such Tantric rites were occasionally married to each other, but in some schools partners were exchanged yearly—a Buddhist should never become attached to any person or thing, was the reasoning—and in others the couplings were totally random.

In some Tantric texts, ejaculation on the man's part is optional, but, in general, release of the semen was strongly discouraged, because "the bliss of retaining and rechanneling the semen is a hundred times greater than that of ejaculating it." More practically, retention of the semen was a form of birth control, and in Tantric schools the ability to control ejaculation was a requirement for admission. Furthermore, ejaculation, according to certain Buddhist tantras, negated everything and could lead to insanity and death. In those texts, semen was equated with *bodhicitta,* the Buddha-mind. Since semen was thought to be the physical manifestation of the Buddha-mind, it was never to be squandered; rather, the semen was to be concentrated in the core of the man's being during Tantric sex, directed through three psychophysical nerves (male, female, and united) up to the crown of the head (the seat of enlightenment)

Tibetan sex charm. Buddhist texts abound with directions for casting sex spells and making charms as well as recipes for aphrodisiacs.

and then recirculated through the body. (It was believed that an advanced Tantric practitioner would bleed semen, not blood, if cut.) A few tantras even prescribed the use of *bodhicitta* pills, concocted from semen and menstrual blood, to clear up the symptoms of duality and incompleteness.[37]

How did the followers of Vajrayāna Buddhism actually apply such teachings?

67

In *Tales of the Eighty-four Buddhist Adepts*,[38] a collection of stories relating the spiritual adventures of Vajrayāna masters who flourished in India between the eighth and twelfth centuries, we have the example of Babhaha, the Free Lover.[39] His story opens with this ecstatic verse:

> Pleasure! Pleasure! Unconditional pleasure!
> Unconditional desireless pleasure!
> Every thought-form perceived as pleasure!
> O what unattainable secret pleasure![40]

Babhaha is described as intoxicated with the joys of sex. A guru instructed him to perceive intercourse as not merely a pleasant interlude but as spiritual communion of the highest order. The guru gave Babhaha this verse to ponder:

> In the lotus mandala of your partner,
> A superior, skillful consort,
> Mingle your white seed
> With her ocean of red seed.
> Then absorb, raise, and diffuse the elixir,
> And your ecstasy will never end.
> Then raise the pleasure beyond pleasure—
> Visualize it inseparable from emptiness.[41]

After twelve years of training in this technique, presumably with a number of partners, Babhaha attained awakening.

The monk Ghaṇṭāpa was another practitioner similarly enlightened through sex.[42] Known as a strict observer of the monastic precepts and as a master of Buddhist doctrine, Ghaṇṭāpa repeatedly spurned the entreaties of the local king to come live in the palace, saying, "Your kingdom is full of vice."

Angered by Ghaṇṭāpa's arrogant refusals, the king and queen conspired with a scheming courtesan to undo the ascetic. The courtesan used her twelve-year-old virgin daughter—"lovely in appearance, with a voluptuous body, a seductive gait, and a sweet voice"—as bait, and the monk eventually succumbed to her charms. United in love, the couple experienced every level of bliss—natural, spiritual, non-dual, and cosmic—and together "transversed the path of liberation to its end."

The couple thus commenced their practice as one body and soul, and the girl bore a child. There was a dramatic encounter with the king, who accused Ghaṇṭāpa as the one being full of vice; whereupon Ghaṇṭāpa proved his sanctity with a series of miracles. He then instructed the people of the kingdom thus:

> Although medicine and poison create contrary effects,
> In their ultimate essence they are one;
> Likewise, negative qualities and aids on the path,
> One in essence, should not be differentiated.
> The realized sage rejects nothing whatsoever,
> While the unrealized, spiritual child,
> Five times poisoned, is lost in samsara.[43]

Both Ghaṇṭāpa and his faithful consort attainted the highest enlightenment in unison and entered the Buddhist paradise together.

These two tales characterize behavior thought to be typical of Vajrayāna masters, but the same text also gives examples of adepts who used abstinence as the key to their practice, indicating that celibacy is an equally valid form of skillful means.

Deṅgipa, for example, renounced his position as palace minister to seek liberation. He humbled himself as a slave, eventually being indentured to the chief of the temple prostitutes. Despite his surroundings, Deṅgipa led a life of chastity for twelve years. One night a customer who happened to stumble on Deṅgipa's hut saw the slave being worshiped by a group of heavenly maidens. Deṅgipa was recognized as a saint, and he eventually converted his mistress and the rest of the girls to Buddhism.[44]

Lakṣmīṅkarā[45] refused to marry the prince to whom she had been betrothed. After distributing her wealth among the poor of her father's kingdom, she cast off her regal gown, smeared herself with ashes, and ran away to the charnel grounds to practice meditation. Upon attaining enlightenment by following the hard path, including the strictest celibacy, Lakṣmīṅkarā taught her disciples to "choose the pure pleasure of liberation over the pleasure of the senses."

The Secret Life and Songs of the Lady Yeshe Tsogyel[46] describes, with all the fantastic imagery typical of Vajrayāna texts, the inner and outer life of a female Tantric adept. Tsogyel was wed to the emperor of Tibet at age thirteen. Three years later, however, she was presented to the Great Guru Padmasambhava for his sensual gratification. (Such generous gifts to a guru were common in Indian and Tibetan Tantra.) Although Padmasambhava accepted her as a disciple, he insisted that Tsogyel first familiarize herself with every branch of Buddhist learning and take ordination as a nun. A brilliant student, Tsogyel quickly mastered all the required texts, and by the age of twenty she was ready to be initiated into the Tantra. During the ceremony the Guru, in his manifestation as Heruka ("the Wrathful One") "took command of her lotus throne with his flaming diamond stalk."[47]

Padmasambhava told Tsogyel, "Without a consort, a partner of skillful means, there is no way to experience the mysteries of Tantra."[48] He gave her the name of a sixteen-year-old boy and where he could be found. After she met him, the two shut themselves up in a cave for seven months and continually experienced the "four joys"— "joyous excitement," "ecstatic delight," "special delight," and "co-emergent delight."

Then, on a completely different tack, Tsogyel embarked on an extended period of solitary asceticism, living as an "ice-maiden" in the coldest mountains of Tibet. During the long nights of meditation Tsogyel was, much like Gotama Buddha, attacked by her inner demons. Foremost was the craving for food and material comfort. Next was intense sexual desire. The most handsome youths imaginable appeared before her, and she had visions of them caressing her, fondling her breasts and vagina, and exposing their sex organs as they teased, "Would you like this, sweetheart?" "How about milking it, darling?"[49]

Tsogyel barely survived these and other torments during her three-year retreat, but she was chastised by her guru for mere role-playing as a hermit, as too proud to admit that she still had human feelings and desires like everyone else. Tsogyel returned to the world and resumed her relationship with her consort as well as taking two more. Following many trials, Tsogyel eventually received full initiation into the Tantra and was transformed into a "Sky-walker," a female adept of the highest order. Padmasambhava said to her, "The basis for realizing enlightenment is a human body. Male or female, there is no great difference. But if she develops the mind bent on enlightenment, the woman's body is better."[50]

For many years thereafter, Tsogyel worked for the good of all—feeding the hungry, clothing the naked, caring for the sick, instructing the ignorant, and "giving her sexual parts to the lustful."[51] Through her skill as a Sky-walker, Tsogyel managed to convert seven men who gang-raped her. She raised their consciousness by singing this song:

My sons, you have met a sublime consort, the Great
  Mother,
And by virtue of your resources of accumulated merit,
Fortuitously, you have received the Four Empowerments.
Concentrate upon the evolution of the Four Levels of Joy.

Immediately you set eyes upon my body-mandala,
Your mind was possessed by lustful disposition,
And your confidence won you the Vase Initiation [sexual
  intercourse].

Apprehend the very essence of lust,
Identify it as your creative vision of the deity,
And that is nothing but the Yidam deity himself.
Meditate upon lustful mind as Divine Being.

Uniting with space, your consort's secret mandala,
Pure pleasure exciting your nerve centers,
Your aggression was assuaged and loving kindness was born,

And its power won you the Mystic Initiation.
Apprehend the very essence of joy,
Mix it with your vital energy and maintain it awhile,
And if that is not mahāmudrā, nothing is.
Experience pleasure as mahāmudrā.

Joined to your consort's sphere of pure pleasure,
Inspired to involuntary exertion,
Your mind merged with my mind,
And that blessing won you the Wisdom Initiation.

> Undistracted, guard the very essence of pleasure,
> Identify pure pleasure with Emptiness,
> And that is what is known as Immaculate Empty Pleasure.
> Experience pure pleasure as Supreme Joy.[52]

Tsogyel also married a leper and served him as a model wife. She died at a great age, and is now venerated as Tibet's top female Tantric master.

Machig Lapdron was another renowned Sky-walker.[53] She was told, in a dream, to seek a consort and "make a union of skillful means and profound cognition."[54] Such a union would anchor and augment the realizations she had obtained while celibate. When she came together with her consort Topabhadra for the first time, the room they were in filled with rainbow light emanating from red and white spheres. They married, and Machig bore several children.

Interestingly, Machig's husband was responsible for most of the child-rearing, since she left home when the eldest was four years old to continue her pilgrimages and retreats. They were eventually reunited, and all the members of her family became masters of the Tantra. (In a different biography of Machig, she was said to have suffered acutely for a time from a daily sexual discharge. A guru diagnosed her sorry state as punishment for indulging in sexual yoga with others without first getting the approval of her principal partner, thereby proving that the Tantra does in fact have certain rules.)[55]

Sky-walkers, also known as *ḍākinīs,* are of many types. One text offers this elaboration of the main kinds of *ḍākinī:*

The Wisdom Dakini is fair, flushed, and radiant. She has five white moles across her hair line, and she is compassionate, pure, virtuous, and devout. Her body is shapely. Coupling with her brings happiness in this life and prevents any fall into hell in the next. The Buddha Dakini has a bluish complexion and a radiant smile. She has little lust, is long-lived, and bears many sons. Coupling with her bestows longevity and rebirth in the Dakini Paradise. The Diamond Dakini is fair, with a well-filled body. She has long eyebrows, a sweet voice, and enjoys singing and dancing. Coupling with her brings success in life and rebirth as a god. The Jewel Dakini has a pretty, white face with a pleasant yellow tinge to it. Her body is slender, and she is tall. Her hair is white, and she has little vanity. Coupling with her gives one wealth in this life, and shuts the gates of hell. The Lotus Dakini has bright pink skin, an oily complexion, a short body and limbs, and wide hips. She is lustful and garrulous. Coupling with her generates many sons, while gods, demons, and men are controlled, and the gates to the lower realms are closed. The Action Dakini has radiant blue skin with a brownish hue, and a broad forehead. She is rather sadistic. Coupling with her is a defense against enemies, and closes the gates to the lower realms. The Worldly Dakini has a white, smiling, and radiant face, and she is respectful to her parents and friends. She is trustworthy and a generous spender. Coupling with her assures one of the continuance of the family line, generates food and wealth, and assures one of rebirth as a human being. The Flesh-Eating Dakini has a dark and ashen complexion, a wide mouth with protruding fangs, the trace of a third eye upon her forehead, long clawlike fingernails, and a black heart in her vagina. She delights in eating meat, and she devours the children that she bears. Also, she is an insomniac. Coupling with her induces a short life, much disease, little enjoyment of wealth in this life, and rebirth in the deepest hell. The Ashen Dakini has yellow flesh that has an ashen complexion and a spongy texture. She eats from the grate. Coupling with her causes much suffering and enervation, and rebirth as a hungry ghost.[56]

Turning again to historical figures, we have the example of Nāropa, the Indian sage.[57] Nāropa married, but his wife magnanimously agreed to divorce when she saw that his mind was set on renouncing the world. Nāropa eventually became the disciple of the guru Tilopa, who during part of his training had functioned as a pimp. Tilopa subjected Naropa to many kinds of disciplines, including one called "Eternal Delight":

"Get a girl," Naropa was told by Tilopa. "She must be between sixteen and twenty-five years old." Naropa was then given instruction in the practice of the Lower Gate, unifying samsara and nirvana with the aid of a sexual partner.[58]

A guru's behavior is never predictable, and one day Tilopa suddenly upbraided Nāropa, a monk, for sleeping with a woman. "It is not my fault," Naropa protested. "It is my penis that is causing all the trouble." In a fit of rage at his inability to control his animal desires after years of practice, Nārope smote his erect penis with a rock until he nearly passed out from the pain. Tilopa then soothed his disciple with a discourse on the essential identity of pleasure and pain![59]

Nāropa survived this and other tests and received full initiation into the Tantra. He passed the transmission to the Tibetan Marpa,[60] who remained a layman all his life and raised a large family. Marpa's star pupil was the famous Milarepa, Tibet's favorite poet-saint.[61]

Milarepa used to wander around stark naked, and once a host of demons attempted to block his path by conjuring up a mirage of huge yoni. Milarepa countered the spell by thrusting out his erect penis and then placing a phallic-shaped stone into a vagina-shaped rock. This spot later became a popular shrine.[62]

This naked saint was constantly being criticized for going about with his penis hanging out. One day Milarepa and his chief disciple Rechungpa were challenged by the clever maiden Rechungma. When she first cast eyes on the two ascetics she laughed with scorn: "An old man and a callow youth . . . exhibiting their bodies, nude and shameless . . . two unscrupulous rascals . . . a pair of Buddhist puppets."

Milarepa and Rechungpa defended themselves with a long poem chanted in unison. Their nakedness, for instance, was explained thus: "Heedlessly exposing our male organs proves that we have no self-made shameful feelings. If one devotes himself body and soul to religion, there should be no reason to feel false shame. It is greed, hatred, theft, and betrayal of trust that are truly shameful, not nakedness."

The maiden and her companions were won over by the performance of the two and begged to be initiated, after apologizing— somewhat incongruously, one would think, in a Vajrayāna text— for being women. "We may have a lower body-form as women, but in the Buddha-mind there is neither man nor woman!" Milarepa accepted them as disciples despite their handicap, and Rechungma and Rechungpa practiced together for a time as "companions in devotion."[63]

On a completely different level we have the story of Sahle Aui.[63] Disgusted and terrified by the world's corruption and impermanence, Sahle Aui petitioned Milarepa to accept her as a renunciate. Milarepa at first tried to dissuade her, telling her to follow the path as a good wife and mother. Sahle Aui wanted none of that:

> At first love is an angel,
> Next a demon, frightening and outrageous,

In the end a fierce elephant,
Who threatens to destroy you.
Thinking thus, I feel sad and weary.

Most men are but credit collectors;
Seldom does a gifted one appear.
First they steal your youthful beauty,
Next they snatch your food away,
Then they pull jewels from your hands.
Thinking thus, I feel sick at heart.
Now I shall devote myself to practicing the Dharma.[64]

Sahle Aui became a lay nun, a powerful meditator, and later a fine master who benefited many sentient beings. She accomplished all this, apparently, without needing a consort.

Like many ascetics, at first Milarepa seemed to disparage women. When offered a fine girl as a bride he responded with scorn:

At first, the lady is like a heavenly angel;
The more you look at her, the more you want to gaze.
Middle-aged, she becomes a demon with a corpse's eyes;
You say one word to her and she shouts back two.
She pulls your hair and hits your knee,
You strike her with your staff, but back she throws a ladle.
At life's end, she becomes an old cow with no teeth.
Her angry eyes burn with a devilish fire
penetrating deep into your heart!
I keep away from women to avoid fights and quarrels.
For the young bride you mentioned, I have no appetite.[65]

Later, however, the beauty Tserinma and her four sisters offered themselves to Milarepa, and he performed the Bliss of Two-in-One with each and took them as consorts.[66] Milarepa declared: "One may reach Buddhahood either as a lay practitioner or a monastic."[67]

Tilopa, Nāropa, Marpa, and Milarepa all used sex in their teaching. But the champion of sexual yoga was the "divine madman" Drukpa Kunley,[68] a kind of Buddhist Tom Jones who was forever inserting his immense penis, "the flaming thunderbolt of Wisdom," into the white lotus-mandala found between a woman's legs. Kunley's biography begins with him in bed with his mother, whom he is trying playfully to seduce. (She had been giving him a hard time about finding a wife.) Furious but unable to rebuff his advances, she was about to give in when he suddenly leaped up and left her alone. Following this incident, he became a wandering Tantric adept.

Wherever he went, Kunley's first question to the local folk was, "Where can I find the best Tibetan beer and the prettiest women?" [69] He was especially fond of young girls with "a fair complexion, soft, silky, warm flesh, a tight and comfortable pussy, and a round, smiling face." [70] Many women found Kunley irresistible—he was said to have had five thousand girlfriends—and often made love to him right on the spot upon meeting, sometimes even in the entrance halls to their homes. Kunley himself had no compunctions about doing it in public and once jeered at an assembled crowd watching him in action, "If you don't know how to do it, here is your chance to learn!" [71] Here is a poem Kunley used to attract one of the *ḍākinīs* he encountered:

> It would seem by the size of your buttocks,
> That your nature is exceedingly lustful.
> It would seem from your thin, pert mouth,
> That your muscle is tight and strong.
> It would seem from your legs and muscular thighs,
> That your pelvic thrust is particularly efficient.
> Let's see how you perform! [72]

Kunley once seduced a sixteen-year-old nun. [73] Later she gave birth to his child but was forgiven by her abbot because the father was "a crazy saint." That created havoc, however, when the other nuns started fooling around, confident that they could always put the blame on Kunley. In Kunley's defense, it was said that each woman who gave herself to him felt more pleasure and satisfaction than she had ever experienced before, and that many went on to achieve Buddhahood as a consequence of that union.

Kunley, a product of the monastic system, consistently exposed the foibles and hypocrisy of monks and nuns who secretly broke the precepts in letter or in spirit. Once when the Karmapa, one of the highest ranking lamas in Tibet, was conducting a public ceremony, Kunley suddenly yelled, "The Karmapa is breaking his vows!" The Karmapa's guards immediately set upon Kunley, but the High Lama called them off.

"He is right," the Karmapa confessed, "I was indeed captivated briefly by the sight of a beautiful maiden in the crowd." Kunley praised the Karmapa's honesty and encouraged the High Lama to resist such temptations (while allowing that he himself could handle it).[74]

On another occasion, an important debate was being held between doctors of Buddhist philosophy. Kunley, instead of bowing to the doctors or to the main shrine, prostrated himself before a pretty young girl sitting on the steps. When the monks protested, Kunley gestured toward the girl's bottom and said, "As the source of all that comes into this world, she—not your arid words or a building of stone—represents the real Mother of Wisdom."[75]

Kunley never stayed in one place very long, but when he did his daily schedule went something like this:

> Dawn to midday: rich food and fine beer
> Midday to nightfall: music and song
> Sunset to midnight: love-play with a consort
> Midnight to dawn: meditation of mahāmudrā[76]

Kunley summed up his life and teaching thus:

> People say Drukpa Kunley is utterly mad—
> In Madness all sensory forms are the Path!
> People say Drukpa Kunley's organ is immense—
> His member brings joy to the hearts of young girls!
> People say that Drukpa Kunley is too fond of sex—
> Congress results in a host of find descendants![77]

> Although your mind may be virtuous and pure,
> The Buddha's Teaching is not accomplished by staying
> at home.
> The teaching of the Tantric Mysteries is most profound,
> But liberation cannot be gained without profound
> experience.

77

> Drukpa Kunley may show the way,
> But you must traverse the Path by yourself.[78]

Free of ties to institutions of any sort, Drukpa Kunley could do what he pleased out in the open; such an option was not available to another of Tibet's "lover-saints," the Sixth Dalai Lama.[79]

Although Dalai Lamas were expected to be models of monastic virtue,[80] Tsanyang Gyatso, number six, had no inclination toward such a life. Tall, handsome, a skilled archer and dancer, a lover of wine, women, and song, Tsanyang Gyatso gave back his vows and lived as a layman. He cared little for pomp, official duties, and politics, far preferring to spend his days at the pleasure garden he had built near the Potala and his nights, in secret, cavorting in the town with his lovers. He may have been influenced by the regent Sange Gyantso, of whom it was reported that "of the noble ladies of Lhasa and those who came from the provinces, there was not a single one whom the regent did not take to bed."[81] There was a storm of protest from his monastic elders when he was found out, but the Dalai Lama refused to change his ways.

> When I'm at the Potala Monastery
> They call me the Learned Ocean of Pure Song;
> When I sport in the town
> I'm known as the Handsome Rogue who loves Sex![82]

On various pretexts, Tsanyang Gyatso was arrested under orders issued by the Manchu emperor of China, and died, in mysterious circumstances, a young man of only twenty-four.

The Sixth Dalai Lama's behavior may have distressed the conservative monastic community, but he had many loyal defenders who maintained that he was practicing sexual yoga in the manner of other Tantric masters and that his girlfriends were all really *ḍākinīs*. One verse attributed to him states, "Although I sleep with a woman every night, I never lose a drop of semen."[83] Furthermore, his love poems, the most popular ever composed in Tibet, are replete with Tantric imagery:

> If the bar-girl does not falter,
> The beer will flow on and on.

This maiden is my refuge
And this place my haven.

Longing for the landlord's daughter,
A perfect ripe peach
Pining away
On the highest branches.

Using astrology
I can easily measure the stars;
Yet intimate as I am with her soft body,
I cannot fathom the depth of her love.

Raindrops can wash away
Love letters written in black and white;
Love written in the heart
Can never be erased.

I seek counsel from a wise lama
To escape from my predicament;
But my mind remains captivated
By my sweetheart.

If one's thoughts toward the Dharma
Were of the same intensity as those toward love,
One would become a Buddha,
In this very body, in this very life.

Mix pure crystal snow-mountain water,
Vajra dew of the dragon demon,
With herbal nectar for the yeast starter.
The bar girl is the Ḍākinī of Wisdom:
If you drink with a pure commitment,
There's no need to experience hell.

Tantric lover-saints like the Sixth Dalai Lama had no trouble making conquests. In was, and still is felt by some women that having sex with an advanced Tantric adept will bring physical and spiritual benefit. In old Lhasa, a number of houses were painted bright yellow, rather than the customary white, to mark places once honored with nocturnal visits by the Sixth Dalai Lama. In more recent times, the Japanese explorer-monk Kawaguchi Ekai was romanced by "a comely little thing" in Tibet. The girl could not believe that he took his vow of celibacy seriously—she had never met a monk who had—and pleaded with him to marry her. Kawaguchi remained faithful to his vows with difficulty. He also expressed surprise at the great beauty possessed by the young consorts of aged abbots.[84]

Although such a Tantra of desire flourished in India and Tibet, its teachings were less appealing to Buddhists in other countries (for reasons to be explained). In Japan, however, there was one sect that went as far, if not further than any Tantric school in India, China, or Tibet:

"The natural coupling of male and female is an adornment of Buddhahood. Sexual intercourse is the highest, not the lowest, form of human activity. It is the source of all religion and all that is best and most beautiful in human culture." That was the message of the Tachikawa-Ryū, a school of Japanese Tantra established in the middle ages.[85]

One of the patriarchs of the Tachikawa-Ryū was Monkan. For more than two decades Monkan had faithfully observed the monastic precepts; he had read every volume of the enormous Buddhist canon, debated with the most learned doctors, subsisted on the thinnest gruel, and spent years in solitude, meditating each day on the vanity of existence. Still, nothing could quench his inner fire and the desire for passionate human love. One night a *ḍākinī* appeared to him in a dream and said, "You must learn to experience the Great Bliss, the union of a man and a woman. Liberation can only be realized through the act of sexual love."

Thus, Tachikawa texts state unequivocally, "Buddhahood resides in the *yoni* of a woman." "If you are afraid to embrace a woman (or man) you will never become a Buddha." "Sexual intercourse is the supreme Buddhist activity." The boudoir, not the temple or the meditation platform, Tachikawa masters proclaimed, was the best, indeed the sole place to win enlightenment.

Tachikawa-Ryū adherents worshiped the Diamond Bodhisattvas of Sex symbolizing these elements:

Desire Diamond Bodhisattva: human desires that can be transformed into the desire for enlightenment.

Sensual Diamond Bodhisattva: the senses by which a practitioner can approach enlightenment.

Love Diamond Bodhisattva: love for Buddha and the Teaching, and the unfolding of compassion and wisdom.

Satisfaction [or orgasmic] Diamond Bodhisattva: the joy and fulfillment of perfect enlightenment.

In the Tachikawa literature, Buddhist terminology is used to describe sex organs and sex acts. One of the school's sacred texts, for instance, was *The Sutra Proclaiming the Secret Method Enabling a Man and a Woman to Experience the Bliss of Buddhahood in This Very Body*. Tachikawa sex philosophers classified sex organs in five types. The five kinds of male sex organs are:

1. *Kongōyasha:*   This is a listless penis, which lacks both drive and staying power. A man with this type of penis is advised to perform esoteric rites to improve performance.

2. *Daiitoku Myō-ō:*   This is a giant penis, long and thick, which frightens women. A man with this condition must learn to control himself and use his monster with consideration.

3. *Kundari Myō-ō:*   This is the kundalini penis, long, vigorous, and full of passion. Matched with an appropriate yoni, this penis can drive a woman wild.

4. *Gonzanze Myō-ō:*   Of average size, this kind of penis puts women at ease. It has great staying power, and can satisfy even the most demanding woman.

5. *Fudō Myō-ō:*   A king of a penis, black, thick, and long. It is a magnificent specimen, which women worship.

The five kinds of female organs are:

1. *Daikoku:*   The dark earth *yoni* that envelops and holds a *liṅgaṃ*.

2. *Mizu-Tembō:*   The water *yoni*, moist, with a small opening and a wide interior.

3. *Ka-Tembō:*   The fire *yoni*, hairy, sweet-tasting, and insatiable.

4. *Fū-Tembō:*   The wind *yoni*, nicknamed the "flying dragon,"

since a man feels as if he is sporting in heaven when he enters this silky tunnel.

5. *Bon-tembō:* The celestial *yoni*, beautifully formed and fragrant. Also known as the "dragon's pearl," this *yoni* has a tight opening and a narrow passage leading to a pearl-like womb. A man fortunate enough to enter such a *yoni* will cry out in ecstasy.

The clitoris was called the *hōjū*, the magic jewel of the Dharma.

The forty-eight positions of sexual intercourse were given such names as "Pure Dharma Realm"; "Sword of Great Wisdom"; "Lotus of Supreme Fortune"; "Crown of All the Buddhas"; "Fulfillment of All Vows"; "Sutra of the Jewel Pavilion"; and "Buddha Fragrance." Ejaculation was termed the "Assembly of Dragon Flowers," while female lubrication was known as "Diamond Lacquer." (Ejaculation, incidentally, was not as widely discouraged in the Tachikawa texts as in Indo-Tibetan Tantric literature; the Tachikawa maintained that ejaculate was a shower of love that contained thousands of potential Buddhas.) The male partner was perceived as Fudō Myō-ō, the Immovable One of fierce intensity who bears the flaming sword of wisdom; the female partner was Aizen Myō-ō, the goddess stained with love, not confused by or afraid of sex but open to all its splendor.

The mandala of the Tachikawa-Ryū was a couple engaged in ritual intercourse. Since the mingling of the cosmic elements was the supreme act of worship, the school denounced autoeroticism and homosexuality as sterile and counterproductive. Participants in Tachikawa rites were encouraged to transform themselves into enlightened beings and were therefore instructed to first manifest the physical form of male and female Bodhisattvas. Tachikawa texts delineate beauty exercises for women practitioners. The buttocks, for instance, can be shaped into lovely half-moons by doing special prostrations and leg raises in which the woman imagines herself walking on air or fluttering through the sky. To enhance the breasts, one should place the hands together in the *gasshō* posture of worship and expand the chest muscles. Men were similarly counseled to strengthen the body and sex organs through yoga and to develop restraint through breath control.

82

Before reenacting the union of Buddha with his Consort, the practitioners thoroughly washed themselves and anointed each other with scent. Their temple was the boudoir, adorned with the best Buddha-image of all—their naked bodies. Intercourse itself proceeded slowly and reverently; it was suggested that the ritual begin at midnight and not reach climax until the first crow of the rooster. During sexual congress, the breath should be harmonized according to the *a* (in) *un* (out) rhythm; the optimum beat is eight (or nine) shallow strokes followed by one deep thrust. "Turning of the Wheel of the Dharma" was recommended as an excellent means to circulate the vital juices, allowing the partners to savor each other's nectar. The instant of orgasm was the moment of truth, a state of pure bliss, an unobstructed blending of emptiness and form, the Jewel in the Lotus—all hail!

Tachikawa apologists claimed that its sole purpose was to elevate men and women from base animals to enlightened beings, a fulfillment of the Buddhist scheme of universal salvation. Most couples, they contended, are caught up in their own delusions and so are usually totally ignorant of each other's real feelings even in sexual intercourse. In the Tachikawa-Ryū, couples were enjoined to always attempt to be in mutual accord, to worship each other as precious jewels and rare flowers.

Unrestrained indulgence in sexual intercourse was never advocated by the Tachikawa-Ryū. Fast days and periods of abstinence were mandated. Sex must be avoided in the following cases: just after menstruation and other inauspicious times; when either partner has skin eruptions; when either partner is in mourning; when either partner has a high fever; and when the female partner is pregnant or in mental distress. Since the sex drive must be sublimated until it can be used properly, yoga exercises for self-control were taught to Tachikawa practitioners. For the Tachikawa teachings to be truly effective, these conditions must be present: the couple must have faith in, and carefully observe, the principles of the school; they must be in total accord with each other, emotionally as well as physically; they must not overeat or -drink; they must not argue; and they must not conduct unauthorized rites or experiments.

Despite the seemingly noble aims of the Tachikawa-Ryū, it was condemned and persecuted by rival Buddhist sects and the conservative samurai authorities. The Tachikawa-Ryū did have some grotesque features—worship of skulls (coated with the effluvia of sexual intercourse, the most potent potion there is) and horse penises, for example—and many of its professed adherents lacked the proper discipline, engaging in orgies and black magic. The Tachikawa-Ryū went underground and was finally suppressed. But it was not forgotten, and the cult still has devotees, in different guises, in modern Japan.

While Tantric Buddhism has many attractive features, most strains contain elements that are very troubling even to those otherwise in sympathy with its aims.[86] It can include justifying outrageous behavior—Padmasaṃbhava is portrayed as once killing all the male inhabitants of a kingdom with black magic and then taking all the women there to wife so that they would bear an army of Buddhist children.[87] It sometimes advocates superstitious nonsense, such as listing magical formulae allowing one to gain entry into any woman's bedroom.[88] Many types of Tantra may even degenerate into the worst kind of perversion—"Feast on my feces, gulp my urine, and lap up the blood from my vagina," for example, is a frequent refrain of ḍākinīs in more than a few Vajrayāna texts. Other recommended activities are outright criminal—"You must slaughter your father, devour him, and then make love to your mother."[89]

Apologists claim that the Tantras are composed in "twilight language," which is never to be taken literally. "Kill," for instance, does not really mean "slay," but rather, "take the life out of dualistic thinking"; and "have sex with all women" means "communicate with all the feminine principles contained within one's own body and mind." It may also be argued that such frightful and disgusting imagery, if that is all it is, is no worse than what psychoanalysts uncover in the psyches of their patients, and that everyone has such thoughts at one time or the other but suppresses them. Nevertheless, the constant preoccupation with the darkest side of human nature seen in certain Tantras can be just as destructive as attempts to totally deny one's sexual and other urges.

Also, despite the safeguards and other precautions supposedly taken by Tantric adepts, abuses were widespread, and more sober Buddhists were obliged to protest:

Perform the Tantric rites literally
And you will surely be reborn as a demon.
It is amazing that Buddhists should act thus;
If practices like yours resulted in enlightenment
Then hunters, fishermen, butchers, and prostitutes
Would all surely have gained enlightenment.[90]

Other sources gave vivid reports of horrifying sex orgies and human sacrifices conducted by self-styled Tantric Buddhists. It appears, for example, that the Chinese Ming emperors were trained by Tantric priests who actually acted out the descriptions of the rites, including incest and human sacrifice.[91] Aged lamas in Tibet were known to have practiced sexual vampirism; they attempted to rejuvenate themselves by procuring the services of young girls and sucking on their tongues, breasts, and *yonis*.[92] And it seems that even the Tantra adepts themselves were occasionally ashamed of their behavior. Langchen, a patriarch of the Nyingma School, tried to hide the fact that a "nun" disciple had borne him two children, and his reputation never fully recovered.[93]

In certain schools, Tantra was in fact purged of its more unpalatable qualities. Shingon, for example, the main Tantric school of Chinese and Japanese Buddhism, retained much of the sexual imagery (though not, with the exception of the Tachikawa-Ryū, sexual yoga) but dispensed with the worship of filth and degradation. And Zen, especially in its Japanese manifestation, was essentially Tantra purified of excess.

4

The Red Thread of Passion: Zen in the Art of Sex

Zen Buddhism is symbolized by a solemn-faced monk sitting in calm repose, seemingly anchored in a tranquil state far removed from the world's frenzied existence. This image of cool self-control, untroubled by the temptations of the flesh, suggests that the sex drive has been thoroughly shackled by icy determination. Indeed, compared with the writings of the puritan and Tantric Buddhists, where sex, pro and con, is a major concern, Zen classics ignore the subject almost entirely, as if it did not exist. The dense, ninety-two volumes of the *Shōbōgenzō* by the Japanese monk Dōgen, for instance, analyzes every aspect of Zen doctrine and practice in numbing detail (there is an elaborate chapter on proper toilet procedure) with the sole exception of sex, an incomprehensible omission, considering the nature of flesh-and-blood human beings.

In the voluminous literature of Ch'an Buddhism, the Chinese form of Zen, too, there are hardly any explicit references to sex. When sex does appear in Ch'an texts, it is almost always in a negative context. Chinese monks and nuns are forever being praised for their steadfast refusal to have anything to do with sex. There are moralistic tales of Ch'an practitioners rising above every temptation. We are told, for example, of a virtuous monk passing this test: The emperor ordered two of his prettiest concubines to bathe the monk to see whether or not he would get an erection. He didn't, and was declared a saint.[1] Even non-monastic Ch'an Buddhists are depicted as preferring the celibate life. Layman P'ang composed this verse about his abstemious family:

> I have a son who does not marry
> And a daughter who does not wed.

The whole family gathers around
And we speak of the Birthless. [2]

"Females are demons. If there were no women in this world every man would be a bodhisattva," was a commonly expressed sentiment among dour Chinese monks. [3]

Although there is scarcely any mention of sex in the orthodox texts, the seventeenth-century ribald novel *Prayer Mat of the Flesh,*[4] subtitled *The Enlightenment Beyond Zen,* reveals the bittersweet attitude toward love and sex among many Chinese Buddhists.

The novel opens with a dialogue between the Ch'an abbot Lonely Summit and the youthful Before Midnight Scholar. Lonely Summit is the ideal Buddhist renunciate, serene and free of all hankering for fame, comfort, or the pleasures of the world. Unlike other monks who secretly have sex the "short way" (with women) or the "long way" (with novices) Lonely Summit is praised as chaste in every aspect of his life. The master urges the twenty-year-old Scholar to become a monk to ensure his salvation. Before Midnight Scholar objects, saying, "I am young and full of passion. Before forsaking the world and finding true peace I wish to search for a woman who will satisfy all my longings." Lonely Summit acquiesces but adds a word of warning: "Then your training will be conducted on the Prayer Mat of the Flesh. I only hope that the grave will not claim you before you see the light."

Before Midnight Scholar embarks on his crusade for sexual fulfillment armed with an extraordinary "jade stalk," the result of a dog penis skin graft. After a series of uninhibited misadventures (among other things, he was involved, simultaneously, with three cousins and their aunt) our Scholar suffers terrible misfortune. Wan, rejected, and disgraced, Before Midnight Scholar appears before Lonely Summit and begs to be accepted as his disciple. The rake Before Midnight Scholar becomes the lowly monk Stupid Pebble and enters the Buddhist Way. Despite his dreadful experience with sex, though, Stupid Pebble is still enticed by the vivid memories of his many former trysts and can make no progress in his meditation. Determined to destroy the problem at its root, he slices off his giant member with a big vegetable chopper in a grand gesture and at last, we are assured, attains peace of mind. (Despite the canonical injunction against self-castration, such a drastic act

Before Midnight Scholar dreams of his past loves during meditation. Before Midnight Scholar, hero of the Chinese erotic classic *The Carnal Prayer Mat* (subtitled *The Enlightenment Beyond Zen*), knew from sad experience the dangers of addiction to sexual pleasure. Yet even as a monk in a remote monastery, he was unable to rid himself of erotic daydreams, recalling his numberless trysts with former lovers. Finally, Before Midnight Scholar availed himself of the most drastic remedy of the puritan elders—he castrated himself.

was by no means uncommon in Chinese Buddhism—a case was reported in this century of an abbot there who cut off his genitalia to still rumors of licentious behavior attributed to him.)[5]

Such extreme puritanical attitudes toward sex seem puzzling when one considers the constant refrain of Ch'an masters to "just be human and follow the dictates of everyday mind." Why is it, then, that Ch'an masters encouraged their followers "to eat when hungry" and "to sleep when tired" but drew the line at "Have sex when feeling randy"?—especially in light of this exchange in a text attributed to Bodhidharma, The Grand Patriarch of Ch'an. Bodhidharma states emphatically, "Lay people as well as monks and nuns are intrinsically Buddhas, and if they see into their natures they become enlightened." A puritan Buddhist objected, "Lay people still engage in sex, so how can they attain Buddhahood?" Bodhidharma's rejoinder: "Once one sees into his or her nature, sexual desire is perceived as essentially empty, and one no longer delights in it as purely physical pleasure. However, even if one continues to indulge in sex, it is performed as a function of Buddha-nature, free of attachment."[6] One may question further, "If Buddha can be a 'shit-stick,' as in one famous koan, why can it not be a swollen penis or a throbbing clitoris?" (One possible reply would be, "If you can remain centered in Ch'an when embracing the most lovely nymph, that applies to you; if not, you must practice restraint!")

Yuan-wu, Sung-yuan, and Tao-chi were the three realists in orthodox Chinese Ch'an who did not skirt the issue of sex. Yuan-wu's enlightenment was precipitated by hearing his master Wu-tsu describing this "little love song" as very close to Zen:

> Time and time again she calls for her attendant Little Jade, not needing her service; she only wants her lover (waiting outside) to be tantalized by her voice.[7]

Yuan-wu reveled in the erotic pleasures of spiritual awakening, as described in this allegorical love poem, which did not exclude sex from enlightenment:

> The incense in the golden burner fades
> As she waits with anticipation behind embroidered curtains.

89

Zen sex kōan. There are a number of sex kōans in Zen. The inscription on this *ensō* (Zen circle) by Taigen says, "Enter from here!" The circle can symbolize the opening by which all human beings enter the world as well as the Void that demands to be filled.

Accompanied by the sound of flutes and songs
Her lover, gaily intoxicated, returns surrounded by friends.
The joys and pleasures of a young man's life
His lady alone knows its sweetness.

Once one of Yuan-wu's former lovers visited his temple requesting a meeting. He gave her this honest poem relating the present sad state of affairs.

Thirty years ago we were of one heart,
Single-mindedly spending the nights in elegant dalliance.

Since then, I've turned old and useless;
Yours too wide, mine too weak![8]

Even though he was personally not hesitant to discuss sex, Yuan-wu followed established practice and refrained from including any sex koans in the compendium *The Blue Cliff Record,* which he edited.

Sung-yuan[9] was ordained rather late in life and knew well how the world actually functioned. One day he addressed an assembly and said in no uncertain terms:

> In order to know the Way in perfect clarity, there is one essential point you must penetrate and not avoid: the red thread [of passion] between our legs that cannot be severed. Few face the problem, and it is not at all easy to settle. Attack it directly without hesitation or retreat, for how else can liberation come?

This was shortened to become the kōan, "Why is it that even the most clear-eyed monk cannot sever the red thread of passion between his legs?" (Legend states that these were Sung-yuan's dying words.)

Regarding sex, Tao-chi was the boldest of the Chinese Ch'an masters. His biography begins with this verse:

> Break the bonds of ordinary love,
> Capture the treasure and become an immortal.
> True renunciation is to realize that the senses are innately
>   pure,
> And that one is an image of the universe.
> Attain enlightenment and you will be liberated from the sea
>   of deluded passion.
> Be settled in meditation and you will transcend the barriers
>   of life and death.
> The respect of kings and the virtue of a Buddha will be
>   yours
> If you bloom like a lotus flower in the midst of a raging fire.

Tao-chi spent his entire career teaching his followers the Zen truth that "flowers are red, willows are green." Tao-chi himself happened to love wine and women, and those things too manifest

91

Buddha-nature. "There is nothing wrong in spending a night together as husband and wife," Tao-chi instructed. "One with a Ch'an mind is above base passion. Human beings have desires which are perfectly natural; one should be like the peach blossoms and willow leaves, which take the deepest pleasure in the bright moon and fresh breezes."

Tao-chi was constantly berating dour ascetics, "Becoming a monk is easy; returning to the world is the real challenge. Too much moralizing destroys the spirit of Buddhism; sometimes it is necessary to refresh oneself in a pleasure pavilion."

> Every day I'm either in a wine shop or a brothel,
> A free-spirited monk who is hard to fathom;
> My surplice always appears torn and dirty,
> But when I patch it, it smells so sweet.

When the emperor, who had hear of Tao-chi's reputation as a Ch'an master, dispatched a delegation to bring the monk back to teach at the court, Tao-chi disappeared. After the party returned without him, Tao-chi surfaced again at the monastery. When asked where he had been, Tao-chi replied, "Drinking in the wine shops and sleeping in the brothels—that is where I practice best, not in the palace."

Tao-chi's death verse was:

> For sixty years I've reveled in confusion,
> Butting my head against barriers east and west.
> Now everything has come together and returned to the
>   source.
> Water flows away beneath the emerald sky.[10]

There is a wonderful inscription on a "Ch'an Circle of Love," reminiscent of a Tachikawa-Ryū sex mandala, in a Chinese erotic manual, which appears to be an answer to Sung-Yuan's kōan.

The Double Lotus

A gentle breeze blowing over the Lotus Pond stirs the pair, resting from the summer heat. They embrace on the meditation cushion and he lets his Ch'an tool slip into her lotus boat. Thrusting with ardor, the Diamond Gate has been opened and all things accomplished. Your body is

Birth of the Buddha. This is a modern Indian version of a classic theme of Buddhist iconography. The Buddha-to-be emerges from the side of his mother, Māyā. Although not a virgin, Māyā was said to have been impregnated miraculously during a dream. This painting vividly depicts the ravishing beauty of Buddha's mother and his subsequent upbringing among an army of lovely wet-nurses and young female attendants.

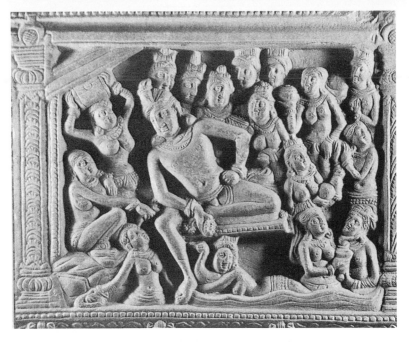

Gotama with his harem. Gotama is shown here surrounded by the voluptuous pleasure girls who catered to his every sexual whim.

Sexual exhaustion. Troubled after another night of revelry, Gotama took a good hard look at the women in his harem. Thoroughly disgusted with their disheveled appearance, Gotama resolved to flee his "cage of gold" and seek the truth as a renunciate.

Gotama on an outing. Sated with the pleasures of the palace, Gotama began making excursions into the city to sample the delights there. Whenever Gotama appeared in public, the local maidens ran to their verandas to catch a glimpse of the handsome young prince. Here the girls of that era are shown naked above and below the waist, clad only in jewelry and tiny girdles. However, it was the Four Sights—a sick man, an old man, a dead man, and a monk—that eventually captured Gotama's attention.

Gotama bids farewell to his wife and son. In some versions of the Great Renunciation, Gotama pauses to take a last look at his chief wife and their newborn son, here shown nursing at his mother's breast. In this poignant portrayal of the scene, the attendants are depicted as moderately dressed musicians rather than buxom harem girls.

The fasting Buddha. From unbridled indulgence in the pleasures of the senses, Gotama went to the other extreme of ruthless suppression of all desires.

The last temptation of the Buddha. Immediately prior to his supreme awakening, Gotama was assailed by doubts and tempted a final time by the tantalizing daughters of Māra, the Buddhist Evil One. Here one of the luscious daughters dances provocatively above Gotama's head, offering to satisfy his every desire and urging him to put off his difficult quest until he is old and no longer interested in sex.

A puritan Buddhist elder. Hoping to emulate Buddha's lofty asexuality, the puritan elders attempted to extinguish the flames of sexual desire, considering passion to be the deadliest of sins for those aspiring to be true Buddhists. Total withdrawal, mentally as well as physically, from the world of the senses was their ideal.

Lord and Lady of Secrets. This is the ideal Tantric Buddhist couple, representing the harmonization of spirit and matter, wisdom and means, male and female. The bliss obtained from such a integration of the womb and diamond realms of existence surpasses all other forms of delight.

a

Even in temples controlled by the puritan elders, we find
countless examples of lush Buddhist beauties, full-breasted
and nubile, adorning the walls; the appreciation of the female form in all its sensuous glory remained even while it
was being officially proscribed. (a) A heavenly maiden from
a Buddhist temple in Sri Lanka. (b) The breasts and pubis of
this figure, from a Buddhist shrine railing pillar in Mathura,
India, have been darkened by the hands of pilgrims who
touched those sacred spots for good luck.

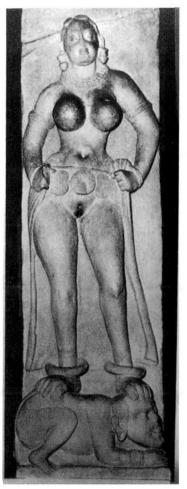

b

Kannon, Buddhist goddess of compassion. In the Far East, Kannon was thought to be able to manifest herself in countless forms in order to liberate human beings from their sufferings. Kannon is said to have appeared to Shinran, one of the founders of Japanese Pure Land Buddhism, and told him, "If one is unable to conquer sexual desire, I shall take the body of a beautiful woman, let him make love to me, and eventually lead him to the Pure Land." The inscription on this painting by Reigen states, "In the midst of the world's corruption, a heart of pure jade."

a   b

Zen and the reality of sex. There is certainly a strong puritan element in many Zen schools
and a common approach to sex among many Zen masters was to either ignore, deny, or
conceal the problem. Other Zen masters, however, were more realistic. Ikkyū wrote that
(a) "Entering the realm of Buddha is easy; entering the realm of the devil is difficult"—
anyone can be a saint in the company of Buddhas; the real challenge is to achieve awakening
in the midst of the world's turmoil and passion. The Ōbaku abbot Zuiun brushed this Zen
phrase (b): "Everything you contact is a place to practice the Way."

Phallic symbol by Hakuin. Hakuin, perhaps Japan's greatest Zen master, was far more reserved than Ikkyū about sexual matters but still brushed fertility charms such as this one for his parishioners.

Double portrait of Ikkyū and his blind lover Lady Mori. The love affair between the Zen master Ikkyū and the minstrel Lady Mori is one of the most famous in Buddhist history. Above his own portrait Ikkyū wrote:

> Within this Zen circle, my entire
>   body is revealed;
> This is really a painting of Master
>   Kidō's reincarnation.
> My blind minstrel sings of love and
>   makes this old rascal smile—
> One tune with her among the
>   flowers is worth ten thousand
>   springs.

Next to Mori's image Ikkyū wrote her poignant poem about their May-December romance:

> In the gap between
> Deep dreams and light sleep
> I float and sink—
> There is no way to staunch
> My flow of bittersweet tears.

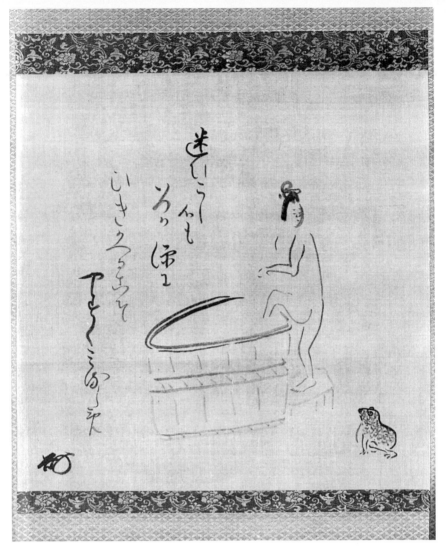

The Bath. In this delightful painting by the Buddhist priest Yuren, the artist (portrayed as a pop-eyed frog) excitedly watches a young lovely step into a bath; she notices the intrusion of the Peeping Tom and looks back with disdain. The frog reflects to himself, "Although I am captivated now, eventually the emotion will subside and my mind will return to its source."

Daruma captivated by a courtesan. Even fierce Daruma, the legendary Grand Patriarch of Zen—who once sat in meditation for nine straight years and tore off his eyelids to remain awake—cannot resist the charms of a young beauty.

Zen "breast" garden, located in Kyoto's Daitoku-ji.

a

Buddhist monks and a nun misbehaving themselves. In the Far East, Buddhist monks and nuns had a perhaps not undeserved reputation for lascivious behavior. Well-endowed monks are the heroes of many ribald adventures, as we see in these two Japanese woodblock prints. (a) An intent monk bringing a courtesan to ecstasy. (b) Although admittedly blasphemous, the seduction of a nun is depicted here with sensitivity.

b

Human sex ensō. Here a Zen circle of enlightenment is
formed by two lovers.

mine, my body is yours. Together we form a perfect, unbroken circle.
Sorrow is painful, it is true, and boundless is the sea of suffering. Yet is
this not pure bliss, the seed of all that is good?[11]

There is also this "sex is good" koan in Chinese Ch'an. A monk
asked his master, "What is Buddha?" The master replied, "A bride
riding on a horse pulled by her mother-in-law." In China, brides
traveled on horseback to their new homes. The women have a vigorous sex life, bear children, and then welcome their sons' wives
into the family—what could be more natural and fitting? In short,
Buddha is life itself.[12]

The Chinese were reluctant to meet the problem of sex head-on,
but the Japanese relished the opportunity to actively contemplate
the red thread of passion.

93

Buddhism was one of Japan's earliest and most important imports and was a central factor in shaping the national character. There was one aspect of that doctrine, however, that the Japanese could not embrace: celibacy. As we have seen, non-attachment to sex was the ideal among the puritan Buddhists of southeast Asia and China. As noted in the previous chapter, the lively Tibetans were far more liberal about sexual matters and Buddhism, but they too maintained huge monastic communities that were committed to chastity. (The Tibetans fiercely resisted attempts by the Chinese Communists to force all monks and nuns to marry.)

In Japan, however, celibacy never had a chance. The indigenous worship of the powers of generation—the gods' supreme gift to humankind—and the unbridled love of love was too strong to be suppressed. Phallicism has always been the norm in Japanese religion. Even today a visitor can witness spectacular penis festivals and join an exuberant procession accompanying a mammoth six-foot wooden phallus as it is pulled through the streets from and to its shrine; spot a stone carving of a "loving couple" (on occasion dressed as a priest and a nun) in intimate embrace along a roadside; or relax in a hot spring where a magnificent rock carving of a male member is enshrined in the bath and where wooden replicas of the same are on sale in the hotel gift shop as souvenirs.

Try as they might, the Buddhists of Japan could not restrain themselves when it came to sex, and in fact did not think it possible. An old Japanese proverb goes, "A man who has never been bewitched by the lovely smile of a woman must be a Buddha made of wood, metal, or stone." Erotic sketches have been discovered on the bases of statues in Hōryū-ji, Japan's oldest extant temple, which dates from the seventh century. Excavations at other venerable temples in the Nara area have turned up more ribald art. Oblivious to the incongruities involved, temple artists used couples tenderly making love as decorative illustrations for stern sutras preaching total abstinence from sex.[13] In the same early era, it is said, the priest-demon-lover Dōkyō enthralled and mesmerized the widowed Empress Kōken with the caliber and talent of his "diamond stalk," nearly managing to have himself named emperor before his fall from grace.[14]

Dōkyō's penis is the subject of a legend in Japanese folklore. The

Aizen Myō-ō, patron of Buddhist lovers. Two forms of Aizen Myō-ō are depicted here in this Japanese woodblock print. *Aizen* means "dyed with love," and this ferocious King of Fire consumes vulgar passions as he refines and purifies the senses. Aizen embraces the universe with tremendous ardor, and when such energy is harnessed it can transmute the basest metal into purest gold.

empress dowager suffered from severe sexual frustration because her vagina was so wide that no man could fill it. A Great Penis Contest ensued, and Dōkyō was declared the winner. Dōkyō's stallion-sized member did the trick for the empress dowager, and thereafter the two were inseparable. The "love paper" containing the pair's sexual effluvia was considered sacred and was dedicated to the gods and Buddhas. After Dōkyō was ousted from power, he supposedly lopped off his penis, the cause both of his triumphs and of his disgrace. His followers preserved the magnificent specimen, had it gilded, and worshiped it as the God of Golden Essence.[15]

Although some of the patriarchs of the early Buddhist sects in Japan achieved status as great monks—typically insisting, as did Saichō and Kūkai, that women be banned from coming anywhere near their monasteries—such continence was too much to expect from lesser priests. Abbot Toba, a Shingon priest of the twelfth century, is admired as being the father of *shunga*, Japan's erotic art characterized by the largest genitals to be seen anywhere. The classic *The Phallic Contest* is one of the works attributed to him. A work of the same period, the notorious *Catamite's Scroll*, a graphic depiction of the homosexual pleasures of priestly love, is a temple treasure of Kyoto's Daigō-ji.[16] The hero of another erotic masterpiece, *The Monk in the Sack*, is a lusty priest who is punished by having his dreams come true. He cleverly seduces three journeying court ladies. Far from being outraged, the women smuggle him into the palace in a sack to continue the escapade. The lonely ladies of the court, ravenous for male companionship, give the well-hung monk no rest day or night, and he comes close to expiring from exhaustion. The tale ends with the monk sneaking out of the love-prison, a sadder, wiser, and thinner man.[17]

By the thirteenth century, Shinran—after struggling with the problem of celibacy for years and being unable to suppress carnal desire through the proscribed course of meditation, fasting, and prayer—was declaring that it was impossible for human beings to remain chaste, so he urged priests to openly marry. Kannon appeared to Shinran in a vision and told him, "Male Buddhists should take a wife; every woman manifests my form."[18] This was the beginning of the married priesthood of the Pure Land schools, which eventually became the largest denomination in Japan—thanks in part to the prolificacy of its clergy. Rennyō, one of the chief Pure Land saints, reportedly wore out at least five wives and fathered so many children (one when he was in his eighties) that people lost count at twenty-seven. (Following the lead of the Pure Land schools, today almost every Buddhist priest—but not nuns!—in Japan marries. One of the last holdouts in modern times, a celibate for nearly fifty years, suddenly married in his mid-seventies and promptly fathered two children.)[19]

Zen priests in Japan continued to hide behind the facade of asexuality, but Ikkyū, the darling of generations of Japanese Buddhists, made no attempt to conceal or deny the red thread of passion that binds us all.[20] Ikkyū was reputed to have been the bastard son of Emperor Gokomatsu. His mother, one of the emperor's concubines, was forced from the palace through court intrigue. Unable to care properly for her son, she sent Ikkyū, at age five, to be raised in a Zen monastery. (Ikkyū appears to have loved his mother deeply, frequently referring to her and her unjust banishment in his poems.) Ikkyū later became the disciple of Kaso, the severest master of the day, and after years of intense training attained awakening.

As an acolyte in the monastery, Ikkyū was introduced, as a matter of course, to homosexual passion. Although the monks did not marry, few were celibate; conveniently, most monks actually preferred the companionship of young boys to that of women (a trait they shared with the samurai of that era). Ikkyū's attraction to women—those who spin the webs of red thread—was too intense, however, and he eventually lost interest in homosexual love:

> Exhausted with homosexual pleasures, I embrace my
>   woman.
> The narrow path of asceticism is not for me;
> My mind runs in the opposite direction.
> It is easy to be glib about Zen—I'll just keep my mouth shut
> And rely on love-play all the day long.[21]

Ikkyū realized that the red thread of passion between men and women was too strong to be severed and that it was dishonest to pretend that it was not:

> Follow the rule of celibacy blindly and you are no more than
>   an ass.
> Break it and you are only human.
> The spirit of Zen is manifest in ways as countless as the sand
>   of the Ganges.
> Every newborn is a fruit of the conjugal bond.
> For how many aeons have the secret blossoms been budding
>   and fading?

Once Ikkyū was summoned to serve as abbot of one of the subtemples of Daitoku-ji, his home monastery. Disgusted by all the sham and hypocrisy around him, Ikkyū announced his abrupt resignation with this verse:

Ten days in this temple and my mind is reeling!
Between my legs the red thread stretches and stretches.
If you come some other day and ask for me,
Better look in a fish stall, a sake shop, or a brothel.

Women for Ikkyū became flowers of enlightenment. Here is his verse on Kannon, the Goddess of Compassion, who epitomizes feminine beauty and love:

Crimson cheeks, light-colored hair, full of compassion and
    love.
Lost in a dream of love-play, I contemplate her beauty.
One thousand eyes of Great Mercy look upon all but see no
    one beyond redemption.
She may even be a fisherman's wife by a river or sea.

Unlike the monks who tried to cover up their sexuality, the girls of the pleasure pavilions with whom Ikkyū associated were frank and totally open. Some of them had the purest motives, having ransomed themselves to support their families, and were like lotus buds blooming in the mire:

The sound of priests piously intoning sutras on the Founder's
    Memorial Day;
How their empty words grate on my ears!
Lost in elegant dalliance
And love-talk, we in the Boudoir of Dreams scoff at grim
    ascetics.

With a young beauty, sporting away in deep love play;
We sit in the pavilion, a pleasure girl and this Zen monk.
I am enraptured by hugs and kisses,
And certainly do not feel as if I am burning in hell!

Stilted koans and strained answers are all you have.
Forever pandering to officials and rich patrons.
Good friends of the Dharma, so proud,
But a brothel girl in gold brocade has you beat by a mile.

Ikkyū once had an encounter with the renowned courtesan known as "Hell." The trademark of this fatally alluring beauty was her luxurious robes portraying the torments of sinners who had fallen into the Hell of Lust. (It was a widespread belief in Japan that it was the customers of whores who went to hell, while the long-suffering girls themselves entered paradise.) When she heard that Ikkyū was in town she sent him this coy note of invitation: "A hermit such as you should be in the mountains, not here in the floating world."

Ikkyū replied with a Zen verse: "Since I have no mind and no body, I am at home both in the mountains and in the floating world." Before actually accepting her invitation, Ikkyū asked around about this particular Hell and was warned not to get burned. He sent an additional note: "Hell is even more awesome than I expected."

She wrote back, "No mortal man can escape the clutches of Hell." For once, Ikkyū decided not to take the challenge and did not descend into this particular Hell.[22]

Ikkyū sketched, in verse, these two portraits of an arhat, a puritan Buddhist saint, lost in a brothel;

> The arhat who has left the world's dust and has no desire
> Finds himself in a brothel surrounded by desire.
> This girl is good, this one is bad—
> It is a monk's task to discern the passionate nature of a devil
>   and a Buddha.

Sexual desire is the pivot around which life and death revolves. It can be suppressed and avoided, as in the case of a puritan arhat, or indulged in, by someone like Ikkyū; the ability to understand the nature of passion, Ikkyū suggests in this first poem, is the quality that distinguishes a Buddha from a demon. Here is the second portrait:

> Emerging from the world's grime, an arhat is still nowhere
>   near a Buddha.
> Enter a brothel once and Great Wisdom will explode upon
>   you!

> Mañjuśrī should have let Ānanda enjoy himself in the
> whorehouse.
> Now he will never know the joys of elegant love-play.

Ānanda, who had been lured into a brothel and was about to succumb when he was saved by Bodhisattva Mañjuśrī's counterspell,
should have been allowed, Ikkyū contends, to test his enlightenment against the vortex of existence. If Ānanda could have maintained his equilibrium in the plane between desire and desireless-
ness, form and emptiness, he would have been a real saint. This is
the meaning of Ikkyū's famous calligraphic kōan, "It is easy to enter
the world of the Buddha, but difficult to enter the world of the
Devil."

For Ikkyū, the passions were the anvil on which true enlightenment was formed. Sexual desire is constantly manifest in myriad
forms, which are, in reality, inseparable from the unborn and un-
dying Buddha-nature. Ikkyū's name means "One Pause," symbolizing a state in which one settles between the flow of passions
and the clear void of enlightenment:

> The lotus flower
> Is not stained by the mud;
> This dewdrop form,
> Alone, just as it is,
> Manifests the real body of truth.

One day Ikkyū was traveling in an isolated district when he happened to see a naked woman preparing to bathe in the river. Ikkyū
stopped, bowed reverently three times in the direction of her sex
organs (reminiscent of the Tibetan Drukpa Kunley's attitude) and
then went on. Several passers-by who had witnessed the scene ran
after Ikkyū for an explanation of his strange behavior. "An ordinary man, and especially a Buddhist priest, would have ogled that
naked woman. Why did you bow to her pussy?" Ikkyū replied
sharply, "Women are the treasure house of Buddhism. They are the
source out of which every being came forth, including Buddha and
Bodhidharma!"[23]

Here is a less serious, almost certainly apocryphal tale reflecting the popular image of Ikkyū, the naughty priest:

Tatsu-jo, the wife of one of Ikkyū's friends, came to the temple one day to complain of her husband's suspected infidelities. Ikkyū said with a smile, "Don't worry about it." They drank some wine together, and Ikkyū began to hold her hand. Tatsu-jo was surprised, and said she would be going. Ikkyū asked her to stay the night, but she became indignant and went home. In tears she told her husband what had happened, but he just laughed and said, "Well, Ikkyū is a real living Buddha, so it is quite all right for you to sleep with him. Go ahead!" His wife unwillingly dressed herself up, painted and powdered herself to the hilt, and returned to the temple.

Knocking at the door, she said in a tiny voice, "I shouldn't have refused you this afternoon. My husband gave me permission to come, so here I am." Ikkyū chuckled and said, without opening the door, "I don't want to any more, thank you. I felt like it then, but not now. Please go back home." Tatsu-jo was furious, but there was nothing to be done, so she went back home and told her husband the conclusion of the story. He clapped his hands and said, "When he moves, he moves, but no one can move him."[24]

Ikkyū's position—"Change base lust into refined love and it is worth more than a mountain of gold"—seems to be very near that of the Tantric Buddhists, but there are certain differences. In Tantric sex, there is always a sense of detachment, an emphasis on transcending the physical form of one's partner and focusing on his or her impersonal, universal aspects. Ikkyū, though, rather than seeing his partners as mere vehicles to be used, actually fell in love with several of them, forming deep attachments to his lovers and their offspring. (Ikkyū apparently fathered at least two children.) Such emotional bonding is rarely found in Tantric texts; an adept is counseled to view his or her partner as an emanation of some higher principle and to keep personal involvement to a minimum. Hence, while *coitus reservatus*, the retention of semen, was standard practice for Tantrics (and Taoists), Japanese Buddhists such as Ikkyū preferred spectacular ejaculations and unabashed intimacy.

This kind of Zen pragmatism, focusing on the concrete here-

101

and-now and accepting things exactly as they are with unflinching realism, is reflected in the following two poems.

> For ten straight years, I reveled in pleasure houses. Now I'm
>   all alone deep in a dark mountain valley.
> Thirty thousand leagues of clouds lie between me and the
>   places I love.
> The only sound that reaches my ears if the melancholy wind
>   blowing among the old pines.

THE DHARMA MASTER OF LOVE

> My life has been devoted to love-play—I have no regrets
>   about
> Being entangled with red thread from head to foot.
> I am not ashamed to have passed my days as a crazy cloud,
> But I sure don't like this bitter autumn lasting for ten years!

Ikkyū's impotence was cured when he met blind minstrel Lady Mori, the love of his life. Ikkyū was hopelessly smitten with her when he was in his seventies (she was apparently in her mid-twenties):

> In what way does my hand resemble Mori's?
> There is no comparison—I believe that she is a master of
>   love-play:
> When my jade stalk wilts, she can make it sprout!
> How we enjoy our intimate little circle.

> Every night, Blind Mori accompanies me in song.
> Under the covers, two mandarin ducks whisper to each
>   other.
> We promise to be together forever,
> But right now this old fellow is enjoying an eternal spring.

> By a river or sea, in the mountains,
> A man of the Way shuns fame and fortune.
> Night after night, we two lovebirds
>   snuggle on the meditation platform,
> Lost in dalliance, intimate talk, and orgasmic bliss.

102

Ikkyū waxed ecstatic over Lady Mori's fragrant yoni and its wonderful taste:

> The tower of love must be stormed by all means.
> Midnight, on the jeweled bed, a bitter-sweet dream.
> A flower buds at the end of the plum branch,
> And the sweet-smelling narcissus between her thighs swells
>   and swells.

> The perfume from her narcissus animates the buds of my
>   plum blossom, sealing our pact.
> The delicate fragrance of the flowers of eros,
> A waterborne nymph, she engulfs me in love-play
> Night after tender night, by the emerald sea, under the
>   azure sky.

> I am infatuated with the beautiful Mori from the celestial
>   garden.
> Lying on the pillow, tongue on her flower stamen,
> My mouth fills with the pure perfume from the waters of
>   her stream.
> Twilight comes, then moonlight shadows, as we sing our
>   new song.

Ikkyū died at age eighty-seven, expressing his regret that he would no longer cradle his head on Lady Mori's lap or pass the nights with her in love-play. To the end, Ikkyū believed that he was following Zen's dictum to just be ordinary in every way, and was faithful to Sung-yuan's teaching that the red thread of passion was a fact of life for all, deluded or enlightened, entangled or not. Ikkyū summed up his life with this inscription on one of his portraits:

> The long sword flashes against heaven.
> My skeleton exposed for all to see.
> Me, I am praised as a general of Zen,
> Tasting life and enjoying sex to the fullest!

In contrast, sex figures very little in the life and teaching of Hakuin, generally considered the greatest of all Japanese Zen masters.[25] Hakuin admired Ikkyū, but his own lifestyle was far more sober, and it appears that Hakuin was never seriously involved with women (or men). There is this single instance of female contact recorded in one of his biographies:

Near the end of his life, the eighty-three-year-old master traveled to a temple to give a Dharma-talk. Upon his arrival, Hakuin suddenly collapsed, racked by violent chills. A middle-aged woman parishioner asked what she could do for him, and Hakuin replied, "Warm me with your body." Removing her clothes, she embraced Hakuin, who then fell asleep for several hours, sweated out his sickness, and recovered.[26]

When he was much younger, Hakuin was accused by a local girl of being the father of her illegitimate child. Given the reputation of Buddhist priests in Japan, no one was surprised by the accusation, and Hakuin said nothing in his defense. When the girl's irate father demanded that Hakuin raise the child, he readily accepted. Hakuin gently cared for the infant without complaint, taking it along on begging trips with him, and silently endured the scorn heaped on him by the villagers. Eventually the girl was stricken with remorse and confessed the truth—a young neighbor was the father, not Hakuin. When the girl's mortified father begged forgiveness for the false accusation, Hakuin replied calmly, "Do not worry about it," handed the baby back, and never mentioned the incident again.

In his writings, Hakuin denounced feudal lords and officials for their addiction to sex and their costly habit of surrounding themselves with vain and frivolous women.[27] He decried the practice of local lords paying small fortunes to secure the services of pleasure girls from Kyoto, girls who would soon be discarded or exchanged for others, and expressed outrage that as much as one-third of the domain's budget went to procure and maintain women.[28] He did paintings of a shrimp, a symbol of longevity, with this bit of counsel: "If you wish to grow old like this, moderate your eating and sleep alone."[29]

Hakuin, however, was no antisex crusader like the Zen priest Munan, who wrote, "No priest or monk should approach a woman. Even though he does not violate the precept, he cannot prevent his mind from being affected by her presence. To approach a woman, therefore, is to initiate a karmic tendency toward the animal state. I make it my practice to avoid women because I am conscious of the residue of animal nature in myself."[30] Hakuin, in contrast, had scores of female disciples, some of them women drawn from the pleasure quarters of nearby Hara, a main rest-and-recreation station on the old Tokaidō road. He also had a sense of humor, one of the key ingredients of Zen. Hakuin wrote, "Those who understand jokes are many; those who understand true laughter are few."[31]

One of Hakuin's more colorful female disciples was Satsu.[32] Girls of that time married around the age of sixteen, but Satsu had trouble attracting suitors because of her homeliness. She was instructed by her parents to pray to Kannon for a suitable mate. One day her father was shocked to see her sitting on a copy of the *Kannon Sutra*.

"What are you doing sitting on that holy book?" he shouted furiously.

"What is the matter?" asked Satsu coolly. "Is there some difference between my rear end and a sutra book?"

Thoroughly nonplussed, the father consulted with Hakuin. The master said with a smile, "You have got a pretty sharp daughter. Give her this poem-koan from me:

> In the night's darkness,
> If you can hear the voice
> Of the crow that does not cry,
> The unborn future [will be clear]
> And you can understand your father's love."

When shown the verse, Satsu was hardly impressed. "What is so good about that? Hakuin is not a whit better than I am!"

Satsu became Hakuin's student, but she was a real handful. Once during an interview she asked Hakuin to explain a difficult point. As soon as he began to speak, Satsu said, "Thank you," leaving the master with his mouth agape.

Satsu resisted attempts to marry her off, but at around age twenty-three she was told by Hakuin, "You comprehend Zen well, but you need to put it into practice. It is best for you to marry, acting in accordance with the natural pairing of male and female. Spirit and form, enlightenment and actualization must be harmonized with the realities of everyday life." In other words, marrying, having sex, and bearing and raising children were all aspects of moving meditation, the kind of zazen Hakuin valued most highly: "Meditation in action is a billion times superior to meditation in stillness."

Satsu followed her master's advice and wed. When she later lost one of her beloved grandchildren she exploded into a torrent of tears. A callous neighbor remarked to her, "I heard that you received a certificate of enlightenment from Hakuin himself, so why are you carrying on so?"

"Idiot!" Satsu shot back. "My tears are a better memorial than a hundred priests chanting lugubriously. These tears commemorate every child that has died. This is just how I feel at this moment!"

Ōhashi, another of Hakuin's female disciples, managed to achieve satori even while serving as a pleasure girl.[33] A lovely, talented young woman, Ōhashi indentured herself as a pleasure girl to support her family when her samurai father lost his position at the death of his lord. Despondent about her fate, Ōhashi was given this sage advice by a monk-customer: "Enlightenment and peace of mind are possible in any circumstance, even here in the flower and willow world. Look for Buddha everywhere and you can attain liberation." Thereafter, Ōhashi assiduously practiced zazen, contemplated life itself as the ultimate kōan, and attained awakening thus:

Terrified of thunder, Ōhashi one day made herself sit on the veranda during a violent storm in order to rid herself of her fear. A bolt of lightning crashed in front of her, knocking her unconscious. When she came to, she felt as if the universe were hers. Hakuin certified her awakening, thereby proving it possible that even a courtesan could become Buddha. Ōhashi was eventually ransomed by a rich patron, whom she wed. Later, with her husband's permission, she became a nun. (Such an occurrence has precedence from the time of Buddha. One of his chief patrons and devoted followers was Ambāpali, the most celebrated courtesan of the day. Following her retirement after many years at the top of her profession, she became a nun and attained recognition as an arhat.)

It is also interesting to note that Hakuin's designated successor at Shōin-ji was Suiō, an Ikkyū-like priest who made no secret of his love for wine and women. While adhering to monastic vows himself, Hakuin gave others much leeway in their Zen practice.

Hakuin was indeed very understanding of human nature. Once a traveling samurai lord stopped near Hakuin's temple and fell desperately in love with an innkeeper's daughter. Despite the promise of love and wealth, the girl refused to leave her aged parents. Hakuin, it is said, carved a little wooden image of the girl for the lord to keep by his side in hope that she would one day consent to join him. Unfortunately, the girl died shortly thereafter and the lord had to be content with memories of his beloved.[34]

An erotic element is, however, definitely present in Hakuin's Zen art. Certain of his monumental one-stroke *ichi* calligraphies have the appearance of huge phalluses, and there is a sketch of a pillar-phallus, a common sight in rural Japan, with this inscription: "Even when the wind blows this doesn't move!"[35] Hakuin did many paintings of *bonseki,* a miniature landscape in a tray. The painting served as both a clever satire on misbehaving monks and as a love charm. Ostensibly, the inscription on the painting says,

> Mr. Bon,
> Are you going to worship
> At Ishiyama Temple?

"Bon," however, is a homonym for "monk" in Japanese; near Ishiyama Temple there was a famous red-light district that was really the main attraction. Thus the inscription also means:

> Mr. Monk,
> Are you going to Ishiyama Temple
> To get laid?

Closer examination of the painting reveals that the miniature mountains on the tray are erect and "fully armed." Hung in the alcove of one's room, such a painting was believed to bring good luck in love and fertility in marriage. (Hakuin's paintings of Fukurokuju, the God of Longevity with an enormous elongated head, similarly served as sex talismans.) One of Hakuin's favorite themes was Mt. Fuji—itself a sex symbol of non-duality—with this erotic little song:

"O lovely Miss Fuji, please shed your veil of clouds, and show me your white skin." This is a delightful way of expressing Zen insistence to "Drop off externals and reveal your true nature."[36]

Hakuin did many paintings of Otafuku, the homely backwoods prostitute with a heart of gold, the Goddess of Compassion in disguise, representing unsullied love and innate purity. In one such painting, Otafuku is shown waiting for customers with a basket of sweet cakes. Hakuin's accompanying inscription hints that the sweet cakes are full of the compassion of Buddha, just waiting for us, but most of us are too poor in spirit to swallow them.[37]

The great Zen master Sengai, on the other hand, had plenty to say about sex. Sengai, too, warned of the dangers of debauchery.[39] He did paintings of profligates ravaged by syphilis and wrote a poem on how to cure blind infatuation with pleasure girls: "Keep in mind the ensuing autumn chill and the deathly frost from which there is no escape."[40] But his attitude toward sex was positive. Here is one of his Buddhist poems, which sums up the way many Zen people feel about love:

> Falling in love is dangerous,
> For passion is the source of illusion;
> Yet being in love gives life flavor,
> And passions themselves
> Can bring one to enlightenment.[41]

Sengai once painted Monju, the Bodhisattva of Wisdom, with an erect penis, adding this verse: "This is a treasure to be fully activated!"[42] A Sengai painting of a couple in sexual intercourse has an inscription that waxes ecstatic over the act:

> This is the original form of interpenetration with the
>   cosmos,
> A Buddhist practice to harmonize the two roots.
> Naked, climb the opposite peak
> And achieve non-dual union.[43]

There is a Sengai cartoon of a man thoughtfully offering his gigantic penis to a lovely Shinto goddess marooned on a lonely island.[44]

A present for the lonely goddess by Sengai. The irrepressible Zen master Sengai frequently took up the question of sex in his Zen paintings. Here, a thoughtful pilgrim brings an offering that the lonely Shinto goddess is sure to appreciate—she is marooned on an island, and a festival in her honor is held only once every three years. This painting also likely served as sex charm for Sengai's lay followers.

Sengai brushed phallic talismans, humorously disguised as mushrooms, for his parishioners. On such paintings he wrote, "Funny, how much this mushroom looks like a penis!"[45] He did a sketch of two golden balls with this inscription: "The reason that we all are here!"[46]

Sengai liked to do paintings about the tale of Kanshin (Chinese: Han-shin), the Chinese official of the Han dynasty who avoided bloodshed by humbling himself and crawling through the legs of a rival general. In Sengai's Japanese version, Kanshin becomes a stout merchant who crawls through the legs of a fierce samurai angered at some real or imagined insult. Reminiscent again of Drukpa Kunley and Ikkyū, Sengai says in his inscription, "Why should

109

Womb sex kōan. The character for "womb" is set off and the inscription by Seigan tells us to ponder its ultimate meaning: "Buddha descended from heaven and was nurtured in his mother's womb, the source of life we must ceaselessly respect." All human beings have been nurtured in the womb of Buddha-nature and have the potential to be enlightened. The womb is also the essential link between the realms of emptiness and matter, sex and spirituality.

Kanshin feel ashamed? Who in this world has not come from between the legs?"[47] Sengai inscribed "Hail to the Lotus Sutra of the Good Law"—the equivalent of "All's well with the world and just as it should be"—on his painting, "Cats in Love."[48] He depicted the God of Good Fortune warming his testicles, explaining, "Warm up the family jewels and keep things cooking."[49]

Sengai was a living koan: One day when he was traveling, a border guard mistook him for a nun. Sengai opened his robe, displayed his manhood, and went on his way without a word.[50] The old master liked to sleep naked, and once a lay disciple on a visit found him taking a nap in that state. The disciple grasped Sengai's penis and put forth the perennial Zen question, "What is this?"

Without opening his eyes Sengai stated simply, "A shriveled-up treasure."[51]

Tangen was Sengai's best disciple, but he had one vice. Nearly every night he would leap over the temple walls and head for the pleasure quarters. Although Sengai was very understanding of human nature (once during an unexpected downpour he sent a novice to the geisha house with an umbrella for Tangen) he felt that such excess would lead to his disciple's ruin. One night Sengai removed Tangen's steppingstone, placed himself beneath the wall, and sat in zazen. Just before daybreak Tangen leaped over the wall, bounced off something warm, and raced to the monastery wondering, "What was that I stepped on back there?" When Sengai did not appear for the morning assembly, Tangen asked the reason. "He has a terrible headache," was the answer. Realizing what had happened, Tangen vowed to mend his ways.

Sengai was very kind to women of all backgrounds. One of his paintings shows a woman earnestly doing zazen, and he added this inscription: "How can the upper root (the penis) be different from the lower root (the vagina)? We need more heroic women!"[52] There is to be no sex discrimination in Zen. Sengai sheltered unwed mothers and took their babies on his begging rounds to obtain food for them. And even more than Hakuin, Sengai was very fond of courtesans and the roles they played in this world, inscribing dozens of portraits of beautiful geisha and bathhouse girls with Zen captions.

The inscription on his drawing of a local courtesan reads, "A pleasure girl is like a razor's edge" (that is, the true test of enlightenment).[53] Inscriptions on similar paintings state, "A great gift, a great gift!" and "[Go ahead,] sleep with them over and over!"[54] On a painting of a beauty emerging from the bath he wrote, "Not easy, not difficult"[55]—indicating, perhaps, that one should try to neither violently resist nor totally give in to sexual passion and beauty but just accept it as it is. Sengai lovingly inscribed this verse on a painting of a beautiful courtesan:

> To conquer this world
> And control the future,

Come, come,
Let me help you become Buddha one time—
Take my hand and sleep with me![56]

Like Hakuin, Sengai believed that Kannon often incarnated herself as a courtesan in order to lead men to Buddhahood, but many foolishly missed the chance because of ignorance or fear:

A face like a peach blossom,
A heart full of love-play,
A powdered face with scarlet lips.
Worth more than any treasure,
The source of life to be greatly venerated.
Hail to Kannon, the Merciful and Compassionate!
But why do the young men around here fear her?[57]

Indeed, monks and courtesans came to be thought of as complementary in Zen. Takuan wrote this inscription on a painting of a courtesan:

The Buddha sells the doctrine;
The patriarchs sell the Buddha;
The great priests sell the patriarchs;
She sells her body—
That the passions of all beings may be quieted.
Form is emptiness, the passions are enlightenment.[58]

Once a young rake brought a scroll to Takuan and requested an inscription. Takuan unrolled it, saw that it was a picture of a naked courtesan in the throes of passion, and without saying a word brushed this inscription on the painting:

Form is emptiness. Emptiness is form;
Willows are green. Flowers are red.[59]

Seisetsu, one of Sengai's Dharma-brothers, composed the poem, "Sporting in the Yoshiwara Pleasure Quarters."

Sometimes true compassion can be found
Sporting in the boudoir of a pleasure girl;

Enjoy then for a time the passion of a young beauty—
On a spring day, peonies burst into full bloom.[60]

In Korea, both the Buddhist clergy and *kisaeng,* pleasure girls, were considered social outcasts by the Confucian authorities. The two groups developed a special affinity—kisaeng supported temples and often became nuns once their careers were over, and it was not uncommon for a monk and a kisaeng to become lovers. The Korean "Monk's Dance" originated with such a love affair:

Chini was the most beautiful and talented kisaeng of her time. She was confidant that no man could resist her, and when she heard of a holy Zen monk who had spent thirty years in the mountains, she set out to ensnare him. Chini was accepted as a disciple, but the monk, Chijok, was constantly on guard. He was able to resist temptation until one rainy summer day when Chini leaped out into the courtyard and began to dance in the rain. After dancing herself into an ecstatic trance, Chini went into the hermitage, took off her clothes, and embraced the now eager Chijok, and the two became one. Chijok returned to the world after this experience and was often seen dancing happily in the streets. When he was asked how he liked living in the mountains for thirty years, he said, "It was wonderful!" When asked how he liked living in the world, he had a similar reply—"It is wonderful!" If the question was, "Why did you return to the world?" Chijok's answer was "Chini saved me from rotting away in the mountains." A dance based on Chini's erotic performance was called "Passion," and one based on Chijok's gay steps, "Emancipation."[61]

The Grand Patriarch Daruma, the universal symbol of Zen, was not confined to a cave or monastery by Japanese Buddhists. *Ukiyo-e* artists adopted him, frequently depicting the stern Zen master in the company of gorgeous courtesans. Such paintings and prints expose how even Daruma, the paragon of self-control and steely resolve, is tempted by the charms of willowy young beauties. In the earliest examples of the Daruma-courtesan theme, Daruma is pictured as merely stealing glances at the beautiful women; later artists, though, painted the patriarch as being completely under the spell of the girls, going so far as having the monk exchange garments with the seductive beauties, thus giving us "Daruma in

113

drag."⁶² Legless Daruma tumbler dolls, which always sprang up
after being knocked down, were originally created to be models of
resilience for children—"Seven times down, eight times up," was
the proverb affixed to them. But Japanese wags quickly nicknamed
low-class prostitutes "Daruma" because they sprang back for more
each time they were placed on their backs.

Although a strict observer of monastic vows, Gōchō, like many
Japanese Buddhist masters, had a soft spot in his heart for pleasure
girls and the important role they can play in Zen. Gōchō added this
inscription to his painting of a courtesan-tumbler Daruma:

> Up and down,
> Up and down,
> I've got a lot of
> Endurance—
> Doesn't anyone notice my true purpose?⁶³

Bokuzan, an eminent Buddhist scholar of the Sōtō Zen school,
on a painting put these words into the mouth of a courtesan shown
confronting Daruma:

> Sitting facing a wall for nine years, big deal!
> I have been doing my work here in the floating world
>   for ten!
> Passions and enlightenment are the two sinews of life,
> But if you are not deluded, they are one—
> Those elements exist together in daily life.
> Cut the red thread and become Buddha!
> For my customers, I turn into the net [of Kannon]
> Hauling them in or letting them sink themselves.
> My job is the same as yours!⁶⁴

In some cases the transformation was complete: Daruma was actually depicted as a young woman complete with symbolic yoni.
This emphasized the fact that enlightenment transcended the male-
female dichotomy.⁶⁵ Another interesting folk custom was the pre-
sentation of a painting of Kanzan and Jittoku to newlyweds. The
two Zen madmen, inseparable buddies, symbolized good-humored

affection and eternal friendship. In erotic *shunga* the two are portrayed as sex organs—Kanzan is "Mr. Prick" and Jittoku is "Mrs. Pussy." An inscription on one such painting states:

> Intercourse is the source of all good fortune;
> Unite, and taste the universe's pleasures! [66]

In Japan, visits to brothels were a regular (if unspoken) part of traditional Zen training. Ekidō, like thousands of trainee monks before him, spent a night in a geisha house. In the morning, Ekidō said to the proprietor, "Last night I was your customer, but this morning I am a priest. Permit me to conduct a Buddhist service for the welfare of all the members of your house." The surprised proprietor said, "This is the first time a monk has not tried to pass himself off as a 'doctor' or a 'student.' One day this fellow will be somebody." The prophecy came true, for Ekidō later was appointed Primate of the Sōtō Zen school. [67]

One day a girl in a geisha house hailed Zen master Mokudō by name. He went inside and discovered that the girl was a childhood acquaintance. The crops had failed one year in their village, and she had become a courtesan to support her family. They talked long into the evening about old times, and then she asked him to stay the night. He paid the fee to the house master, and the girl spread out the bedding. She pulled back the covers and said, "Come join me. No one will know." Mokudō replied, "It is kind of you to invite me, but right now I'd rather do zazen. Your present occupation is to sleep with customers, and my current job is to sit in meditation. Let's leave it at that." [68]

Enthusiastic trainee monks were favorites of the girls in the pleasure quarters. In Kyoto, one novice spent so much time in the pleasure quarters that his name became a generic term for any monk on a spree. [69] The handsome Tekisō was pursued by many geisha and, abandoning his robes, lived with one for some time. One day he saw a procession of Zen monks on their begging rounds and sighed, "Oh, how I would like to give it one more try!" His lover immediately prepared his things, kissed him gently, and sent him on his way. After Tekisō became abbot of a large temple, he gave the courtesans from the local brothel calligraphy lessons, and whenever he held a service for them, after the chanting Tekiso would join the girls in song and dance.[70]

Zen masters were also capable of romance. Late in life Ryōkan[71] fell in love with the beautiful young nun Teishin. Although it appears that their relationship remained platonic, the two exchanged a series of tender love poems. When Teishin met Ryōkan for the first time she composed this verse:[72]

> Was it really you
> I saw,
> Or is this joy
> I still feel
> Only a dream?

Ryōkan's reply:

> In this dream world
> We doze
> And talk of dreams—
> Dream, dream on,
> As much as you wish.

There was also this exchange:

> Here with you
> I could remain
> For countless days and years,
> Silent as the bright moon
> We now gaze at together.
>
> (Teishin)

> If your heart
> Remains unchanged,
> We will be bound as tightly
> As an endless vine
> For ages and ages.
>
> (Ryōkan)

When Teishin failed to visit Ryōkan, he sent her this plaintive poem:

Have you forgotten me,
Or lost the path here?
Now I wait for you
All day, every day,
But you do not appear.

Teishin wrote back, complaining that her involvement with
worldly affairs kept her away:

The moon, I'm sure,
Is shining brightly
High above the mountains,
But gloomy clouds
Shroud the peak in darkness.

Ryōkan sent back this advice:

You must rise above
The gloomy clouds
Covering the mountaintop
Otherwise, how will you
Ever see the brightness?

Snowed in all winter, Teishin was not able to visit Ryōkan until
the spring thaw. When he saw her, Ryōkan exclaimed:

In all of heaven and earth,
There is nothing
More precious
Than a visit from you
On the first day of spring.

He added:

The Way of Buddha
Is not something
You can touch with your hand;
Realize this,
And all will be well.

One summer day, Teishin called on Ryōkan and found that he was out. She left this poem for him:

> I missed seeing you
> When I visited your hermitage,
> But the little hut
> Was full of the fragrance
> Of a lotus flower.

Ryōkan sent this response:

> Indeed, all the decoration
> I need
> Is a single lotus flower—
> When you see one,
> Think of me.

Because of his black robe and sunburnt complexion, Ryōkan was nicknamed "Crow" by Teishin and her friends. (In the Far East, the crow is a symbol of eternal love.) Highly pleased, Ryōkan came up with this verse:

> Free as a bird
> To go wherever I please,
> From tomorrow
> I will take the name "Crow"
> Given to me by my friends.

Teishin added at once:

> When a mountain crow
> Flies to his home,
> Shouldn't he take along
> His soft-winged
> Little darling?

Ryōkan replied with a smile:

> I'd love to take
> You anywhere

I go,
But won't people suspect us
Of being lovebirds?

Teishin rushed to Ryōkan's side when he was on his deathbed.
When she arrived, Ryōkan summed up his love for her:

"When, when?" I sighed.
The one I longed for
Has finally come;
With her now,
I have all that I need.

Speaking of Ryōkan, there is a delightful story regarding one of
his impromptu compositions. Ryōkan's calligraphy was highly valued, and people were forever pestering him for samples of his brush-
work. Ryokan disliked such requests because many only wanted
the calligraphy in order to impress others, and he usually put
people off by telling them that he would do something "later."
Ryōkan loved to play the board game *go,* and often the stakes involved a piece of his calligraphy. Ryōkan once lost a game, and his
shrewd opponent eagerly awaited his prize. Instead of the flowery
Zen phrase that he expected, however, he received this calligraphic
statement from Ryōkan:

Picking persimmons—
My testicles are frozen
By the autumn wind! [73]

Ryōkan loved to join in the all-night dances of the Summer Bon
festival, but since he was a monk he had to disguise himself by
wearing a big kerchief and a women's kimono. All the villagers
knew, of course, that it was Ryōkan, and one year several of the
men decided to tease him. "Who is that charming girl?" they whispered among themselves just loudly enough for Ryōkan to hear.
"She certainly is a good dancer!" Extremely pleased, Ryōkan lost
himself in the role of female dancer, swaying to and fro with feminine grace.

119

There were not many women Zen masters in Japan, but Eshun was one of the sharpest, male or female.[74] Because she was famed throughout the land as an unrivaled beauty, her brother, the abbot Ryōan, was taken aback when she asked to be ordained a nun. Ryōan put her off, saying, "A woman's place is in the home. You can practice Buddhism perfectly well as a lay believer. Besides, you are too good-looking. The trainee monks could never control themselves." A few days later Eshun returned, this time with her head shaven and her face disfigured by the red-hot coals that she had applied to her skin.

Seeing her determination, Ryōan relented, but even with scars on her face and baggy robes hiding her figure, Eshun was a knockout. A young monk fell for her and slipped a love letter into the sleeve of her kimono. Eshun wrote back, "I accept your proposal, but since we are both under vows we will have to meet in secret. I will let you know the time and place."

The next time the community gathered to hear the abbot give a sermon, Eshun suddenly appeared in the main hall without a stitch of clothing. She stood before the amorous monk and said to him, "If you really love me, embrace me now!" The monk fled from the temple, forever shamed, as the abbot and the rest of the monks looked on dumbstruck.

On another occasion Ryōan decided to send Eshun as his representative to a special congress to be held in the ancient monastery of Engaku-ji in Kamakura. When some of the monks there heard the news, the scoundrels devised a crude trick to test the nun. Not long after her arrival at Engaku-ji, a monk leaped out in front of Eshun, exposing himself and exclaiming, "This old monk's thing is three feet long! How about it?" Without a moment's hesitation, Eshun opened the front of her robe and replied, "This nun's thing has no bottom!" and brushed past him.

A somewhat similar episode was used as a kōan by Suzuki Shōsan, a proponent of samurai Zen. There was a very sharp laywoman named Mujaku who lived in a certain monastery. The master there sent all the senior monks to her for the acid test. Man'an, an older priest of some distinction, went for a Zen encounter. Mujaku called him into her room, and when Man'an entered he found her lying there stark naked. He pointed to her pubis and demanded to know, "What is that? A portal to the world?"

Mujaku responded, "All the Buddhas of the past, present, and future, all six Zen Patriarchs, and all venerable monks came forth from here!"

"Can an old monk like me go back there or not?" Man'an asked.

Mujaku announced, "Jackasses get nowhere here," turned toward Man'an, spread her legs, and flashed him. Man'an, red-faced and sheepish, beat a hasty retreat.

Shōsan's kōan was: "What would you have said in answer to the question, 'Can an old monk like me go back there or not?'"[75]

A real Zen master never shrinks from the subject of sex, and Tesshū, the valiant, enlightened layman of the Meiji era, tackled the problem head-on.[76] As a young man Tesshū was both fascinated and perplexed by the difference between male and female, self and other. Hoping to bridge the gap, Tesshū embarked on the "ascetic discipline of sexual passion," vowing to make love to every courtesan in Japan. The handsome, fiercely determined Tesshū mesmerized the girls in the gay quarters, and a few of them went so far as to refuse to be ransomed so they could continue to meet their tireless lover. (Later, when Tesshū became a famous Zen master, his calligraphy was prominently displayed in the alcoves of geisha houses in the pleasure quarters.) Tesshū's wife finally objected to his endless nights out, rejecting his explanation that his trips to the brothels were an essential part of his Zen training. She demanded that he stop, and he did; but later he remarked, "Even following satori, the fundamental problem of sex persisted. Not until my forty-ninth year (Tesshū died at age fifty-two) was I able to transcend sexual passion."

A friend suggested that Tesshū was just getting old. "No," Tesshū said. "What you mean by sexual passion is physical lust. I was over that by my mid-thirties. If one cannot penetrate the nature of sexual passion—the root of samsara and the basic life force—to its source, one's enlightenment is worthless." Sex is the supreme kōan.

One of Tesshū's married disciples once said to him, "In order to really practice Zen, it is necessary to cut off sexual passion."

"That's quite an exalted state you are aiming for," laughed Tesshū. "Sexual passion is the root of all existence. How do you propose to cut it off?"

"By separating from my wife and keeping totally away from all other women; then sexual temptations will not arise."

'That's rather selfish, isn't it? What will happen to your wife, a faithful companion for twenty years? That is no way to cut off sexual passion—that is merely avoiding it."

"Then what should I do to eradicate sexual passion?"

'Throw yourself into the world of sexual passion, exhaust its possibilities, and then you will find release. Love your wife with all your might and seek enlightenment in the very midst of life—that is the meaning of Zen."[77]

In his book *Zen Activity*, Mokurai, longtime abbot of Kyoto's Kennin-ji, relates a number of interesting anecdotes about sex and Buddhism.[78] Mokurai compared Zen training to entering a gourd. The opening is extremely narrow, so practitioners must keep themselves under tight control in order to squeeze through. Thus Mokurai praised the example of Nantembō, who as a trainee monk had raging erections whenever visions of beautiful women appeared before him during Zen meditation. Nantembō cursed the erections and suppressed the enticing fantasies by sheer force of will.[79] Nantembō himself told this tale: "Once I was traveling on a ship, and at one port my fellow passengers summoned a bevy of whores to entertain them. They got a girl for me, too, but I paid her off and told her to leave. The quarters were very cramped, and I had no choice but to place myself right in the center of the orgy and do zazen. It was really a trial!"[80]

Then there is the well-known story of two trainee monks who, while traveling, came to a river and met a young woman who was unable to cross because of the strong current. One of the monks said to her, "Hop on my back and I will carry you across." The girl hitched her kimono all the way up and climbed onto the monk's back, and he deposited her safely on the opposite shore.

The monks went on their way, but the other one protested, "What were you doing back there? You know how strict our master is and that we are not allowed to touch women!"

"What is the matter with you? Are you still carrying that girl? I left her back there on the bank," the other replied.[81]

Mokurai also mentioned the love letter the famous abbot Musō received from one of Kyoto's loveliest geishas:

> For just one night,
> Let your vow of chastity lapse—
> Is not a cloudy stream
> Made clear again
> By the flow of the waterfall?

Musō declined with this verse:

> My life will be
> In all the more danger
> If I let this dewdrop body
> Fall into your hands—
> A chill wind stings the autumn clover.[82]

Once through the narrow gate, though, the gourd opens widely and we have lots of room in which to roam.

Mokurai knew a monk called Tangai, who restored a monastery in Minō. The temple lent money to a certain geisha house run by one of its parishioners. When the house was unable to repay the loan, Tangai accepted instead the services of a young geisha, in effect ransoming her from the pleasure quarters. Tangai was quite open about their relationship, and the girl accompanied the abbot everywhere—to the main hall, to the zendo, to the abbot's quarters. She was an excellent attendant, and Tangai grew fond of her; she continued to live with him long after the debt was paid.[83]

Another one of Mokurai's abbot friends was sent by his parishioners to Kyoto to buy a new Buddha image for their temple. The abbot, overcome by the attractions of the elegant capital, spent all the money in the Shimabara pleasure quarters. He returned to his temple and unveiled the new image, a gaudy Kyoto courtesan doll. "Unlike an impassive lump of metal or wood, this Buddha statue knows firsthand the bittersweet nature of this floating world," the abbot told his parishioners. They agreed, and ordered similar dolls for their own home altars.[84]

Mokurai concurred: "So many Buddhists believe that it is necessary to seclude oneself in the mountains in order to really practice Zen. That is a great error. One should be able to do Zen even in a brothel. Those who are agitated by sex should place the blame squarely on themselves and not accuse others of causing temptation. I have known plenty of courtesans who understood Zen better than most trainee monks.[85] I did not realize this myself when I was young. Once I was asked to find a priest for a temple in the country. I recommended a monk who was known for his strong aversion to women and his strict vegetarian, teetotalling diet. To my surprise, the parishioners were not at all pleased with my choice. 'A young monk who detests women and good food and drink? There must be something wrong with him!'"[86]

To be a lifeless bump on a log is not the Zen ideal. There was a layman who had high regard for a certain Zen priest but feared that the monk was becoming stone-hearted, too indifferent to normal emotions. People in Japan bathe together, and one day as the layman and the monk entered the bathhouse the layman reached around from behind and grabbed the monk by the testicles.

"Ouch!" the monk cried out in pain.

"Good," the layman smiled. "You are still human."[87]

Mokurai summed up Zen training in this way: "When you are a novice, keep a firm hold on your balls; when mature, let them swing freely like a bull's!"[88]

Not long ago in Kyoto, there was a priest known as Bobo Rōshi, "Friar Fuck." A model trainee for twenty years, Bobo was getting nowhere in his practice and one day, confused and disheartened, he decided to visit the Shimabara pleasure district. At the instant of his first orgasm in years, Bobo underwent a wrenching satori. His experience was recognized as genuine and, it is said, he continued to visit Shimabara every once in a while to deepen his understanding of Zen. Appropriately, Bobo Rōshi's grave is marked by a giant stone phallus.[89]

Let us conclude this section with a sex kōan that Zen Buddhists have been pondering for centuries:

An old woman built a hermitage for a monk and supported him

for twenty years. One day, to test the extent of his enlightenment, the old woman sent a young girl to the hut with orders to seduce him. When the girl embraced the monk and asked, "How is this?" the monk replied stiffly, "A withered tree among the frozen rocks; not a trace of warmth for three winters." Hearing the monk's response, the old woman chased him out and put the hermitage to the torch.[90]

Why?

5
Buddhist Love, Marriage, and Sexual Morality

Marriage in Buddhism is an open question—there is no single standard of behavior. In old Tibet, often characterized as the Buddhist civilization par excellence, every type of marriage (monogamy, polygamy, polyandry) was allowed. Couples, especially Tantric masters and their consorts, could live together openly without formal marriage vows, prostitution was tolerated, and celibacy was a valid option for those who wished to renounce the married state altogether.[1] Marriage in Tibet (as in the rest of Buddhist Asia) was essentially a secular affair, and attempts were not made to define the proper kind of marriage for lay Buddhists.

The majority of marriages in Tibet were arranged. The main form of marriage was, apparently, monogamy, but polyandry and polygamy were also widely practiced. Virginity was generally not expected of the bride, except for marriages among the nobility where blood lines were important. (There is considerable evidence that during certain periods in parts of central and southeast Asia Buddhist priests deflowered soon-to-be-wed virgins as a "sacred duty."[2]) In polyandrous unions, which were more common, one wife would share several brothers, who usually took turns absenting themselves on business trips, pilgrimages, and the like so that just one husband would be with her at a time. When a child was born, the eldest brother was considered the father, even in cases where it was clear that he was not. In polygamous marriages, a man would usually marry two or three sisters. There were also cases of what might be termed "polygyandrous" unions, that is, two sisters jointly marrying two brothers, and situations in which a father and son would take the same woman to wife.[3] Tibetan marriages were

126

quite complex, and there is record of a mother being the sister-in-law of her own daughter.[4] While not condoned, incestuous unions between brothers and sisters occurred on occasion—a famous lama, for example, was openly acknowledged to be the product of an incestuous relationship between a monk and his sister.[5] Divorce was permitted and comparatively easy to obtain by either party.

Unlike those of most Asian countries, Tibetan women evidently enjoyed de facto equality with men. A traveler from Japan who visited old Tibet remarked on how independent Tibetan women seemed, maintaining their own sources of income and savings and allowed to take an outside lover if they so desired. The Japanese traveler, accustomed to the obedient women of his native land, recorded with some shock the scene of a Tibetan wife publicly heaping abuse on her cowering husband, who was on his knees before her abjectly apologizing for some transgression.[6]

Kawaguchi also reported that the hospitable Tibetans would offer their wives or other female members of the household for the pleasure of travelers and other unexpected guests.[7] This has been disputed by Harrer, however, who states that such a thing never happened to him during years of travel all over Tibet. On a few occasions, he was told to avail himself of the charms of a young servant girl, but the girl would still have to be courted and won over.[8]

Harrer made a number of interesting observations regarding Tibetan sexual customs. He met women who lived simultaneously with two or three husbands.[9] In one case there was a woman who was wife to three brothers. She seemed perfectly content, but one day a traveler stopped at their tent, and she fell in love with him. Without a second thought, the couple eloped to Lhasa.[10] Harrer mentions a Tibetan noblewoman who was "the first woman in Tibet to refuse to marry her husband's brothers simply because it was the traditional custom," and her crusade for human rights.[11] Widows and widowers could marry again after observing a short period of mourning.[12] Prostitutes were common in Lhasa, Harrer wrote, and venereal disease widespread.[13] He was amazed at the cavalier fashion with which the Tibetans treated sex. All of his Tibetan male friends, including high-ranking abbots, continually advised him to take at least one female companion.[14] Homosexuality was an accepted practice in the monasteries.[15] A monk and a nun transgressed their vows, the nun became pregnant, and when the child was born they murdered it. The guilty pair were found out and sentenced to be flogged and exiled for their grave crimes. During the public flogging, however, the crowd pleaded with and then bribed the authorities to reduce the number of lashes. Onlookers also showered the pair with gifts of money and food, getting their exile off to a comfortable start.[16]

A recent autobiography by a Tibetan noblewomen, an ardent life-long Buddhist, provides us with a perspective on Tibetan marriage customs.[17] The offspring of a "nun" and a powerful government official, this Tibetan lady was first married at age sixteen to a man who had already taken two of her older sisters to wife. She was reluctant to marry but decided to do so because of difficult family circumstances (her father had been assassinated); also, her husband promised to release her if she found a suitable younger man.

After bearing her first husband a child, she was introduced to a young diplomat as a prospective mate. When they decided to wed, she discontinued conjugal relations with her first husband in order not be pregnant at the time of the second marriage ceremony. (It is not clear whether or not she obtained an official divorce from her first husband.) Her young child was left with the first husband to raise. She grew fond of her new husband and made a personal vow of monogamy, without requesting a similar vow from him. At any rate, he took no more wives, and the pair spent their life together in monogamy.

As we can see from the Tibetan example, it is clear that the type of sexual relationship an individual enters into has no direct bearing on his or her ability to practice Buddhism.

Regarding the practical side of sex and marriage, the Tibetans were realistic. Tibetan doctors, for example, usually questioned patients in detail about their sex lives before making a diagnosis. They saw an active sex life as important for good health and general well-being and frequently prescribed sex as a remedy for certain disorders.[18] Undue suppression of sperm, for example, can result in penile diseases, cutaneous swelling, fever, palpitation of the heart, painful limbs, enlarged testicles, difficulty in passing urine, impotence, bad eyesight, and weakening of the internal organs![19] One Tibetan medical text recommends the following schedule for sexual intercourse: two or three times a day in winter (sperm count increases in that season); every two days in spring and autumn; once every fifteen days in summer.[20]

In the biography of Yuthong, one of the pioneers of Tibetan medicine, there are several interesting sections regarding sex. Yuthong, a celibate monk for nearly eighty years, had a vision in which a dākinī counseled, "In order to become a true physician you must take a consort." Yuthong married a beautiful sixteen-year-old maid (of course!) and fathered a boy at age ninety and a girl (whom he named "joyful") at age ninety-five.[21]

Yuthong had a nun patient who was tormented by sexual desire; she consulted him when the radish that she was using for a dildo broke off inside her. Yuthong instructed her on how to redirect her sexual impulses, but it was no use. Finally he simply told her to sleep with a man and forget about being a nun. She followed his prescription and was cured completely.[22]

An ascetic monk came to Yuthong complaining of extreme fatigue, splotchy skin, swollen limbs, acute headaches, and difficulty breathing.

"What is the matter with me?" he cried in anguish.

Yuthong replied, "By not drinking beer you have become emaciated and developed dropsy; by staying out of the sun you have damaged your skin; by not eating salt you have weakened your bones; by avoiding women you have allowed your penis to shrivel. Have a good dose of beer, sunlight, salt, and women, and you will recover."[23]

Similarly, during the annual Monlom festival in Lhasa there was an unofficial "dispensation" for monks[24] and nuns, and many of them sated themselves with beer and sex. And when asked by a foreigner why Tibetans freely donated their children to monasteries, a father replied with a smile, "We are simply returning the sons who were fathered by the monks with our wives."[25]

As related in detail in chapter 2, a sizable portion of Buddhist literature is devoted to denigrating marriage as a fate worse than death. In reality, however, even puritan Buddhists recognized the value of marriage. As a young man in his twenties, a western Buddhist received this sage advice from a Chinese elder:

Yes, Buddhism enjoins chastity on adepts for the truly spiritual life—monks and very strict laymen. All the same, it can do you more harm

129

than good. Most young men who keep themselves strictly chaste find themselves visited by sexual fantasies and torturing longings which are worse for them than occasional visits to the flower-houses, while marriage is far better still. . . . Perfect chastity is dangerous, unless you really have mastered such longings. Buddhism does not enjoin enforced chastity, which is the road to madness, but the gradual mastery of desire. . . . That is why I wish you would consider getting married. . . . Do accept this friendly warning from one Buddhist to another—the conquest of desire's modes of expression is worthless until you have conquered desire itself. To enforce chastity upon yourself is insufficient and exceedingly dangerous besides. You must aim at so mastering your desires that they have no power to torment you. This, unless you are a budding Bodhisattva, will take you so long that it is far, far better for you to get married in the meantime. [26]

And even though puritan Buddhists did their best to describe love and marriage in the bleakest possible terms, tender love stories and examples of happy marriages are found everywhere in the Buddhist tradition. In addition to those noted previously, here are a few more Buddhist tales of love and romance:

In Buddha's time there was the devoted couple known as "Nakula's parents." The father once declared to Buddha that ever since he had taken her as a child bride, he had not transgressed against his wife, even in thought—"My sole wish is to be united with her forever, in this world and the next." When Buddha heard the wife echo the same sentiments regarding her husband, he announced to his followers:

"This husband and wife are indeed well-matched—well-matched in faith, well-matched in virtue, well-matched in generosity, well-matched in goodness, well-matched in wisdom. A perfect pair and a wonderful example of wedded bliss, surely they will be together for eternity, enjoying great felicity." [27]

One of Buddha's followers was blessed with a devoted wife who was good and virtuous as well as beautiful and charming. On a journey the couple was waylaid by bandits. The gang leader threatened to kill the husband and carry off the wife. The woman told the bandit chief defiantly, "If you harm my husband, I will kill myself on the spot." Seeing that there was no chance of getting their way, the bandits let the couple go.

Buddha was told of the incident and said to the husband, "You are very fortunate to have such a good wife. She also saved my life in a previous incarnation. I was an elephant king and she was my mate. I was determined to destroy a monster crab that was terrorizing our herd, but it caught my leg with one of its claws. All the other elephants fled in panic, and I was being pulled down into the river. 'Don't leave me!' I yelled out to my mate. 'I will never leave you, noble husband, the one I have adored for all these years,' she reassured me. She then tricked the crab into slightly loosening its grip, and I was able to crush the monster."

Buddha concluded, "With such a fine woman as your wife you are assured of eternal happiness and joint attainment of enlightenment."[28]

Another loving wife was Sujātā—". . . fair and lovely, as beautiful as a divine nymph, as graceful as a twining creeper, and as ravishing as a sylph." She and her husband "dwelt together in joy, unity, and oneness of mind." An evil king framed the husband in order to seize Sujātā; fortunately, the gods answered the pleas of the good woman and both she and her husband were saved. In Buddhism, too, true love prevails.[29]

There is this instance of a husband and wife renouncing the world together: When the husband (Buddha in a previous incarnation) abandoned the world to become an ascetic, his beautiful wife insisted on joining him. He tried his best to dissuade her, saying, "You have already proved your love and devotion to me; besides, the life of a homeless ascetic is extremely trying, and one on that path is cautioned to stay away from members of the opposite sex." She protested that she could not live without him, so he relented, and they retired to the forest together.

One day they were meditating together in a lovely grove.

> It was early spring when nature is most vibrant. All around, tender young shoots reached toward the sun while intoxicated bees hummed dreamily and preening cuckoos sang out happily. Lotus filled ponds glistened in the sun; soft breezes carried the fragrance of a thousand blossoms. It was like a playground of the god of love, full of light and sweetness.

The local king, enjoying an outing in the forest, happened to come across the ascetic couple and, not surprisingly, given the ambience, became totally enamored of the woman. The king had her

131

seized, but the unruffled behavior of the husband ascetic, and a penetrating discourse on the dire consequences of losing one's self-control, saved the day. The woman was released, the king became a disciple of the ascetic, and once again everyone lived happily ever after.[30]

Once a king had an argument with his queen, Jasmine Bride, and they spent the night apart. When informed of the trouble, Buddha related an edifying tale of eternal love:

"Long, long ago, you and your queen were water sprites. One day I caught sight of you two along the riverbank embracing and kissing passionately. Suddenly, much to my surprise, you both burst into tears, wailing most piteously. When I asked the reason for such behavior, the female sprite sobbed, 'One night we slept apart, loveless, full of anger and bitterness. We reconciled the next morning, but the pain of that one night of separation still causes us much grief and we recall it every day, even after seven hundred years. When two hearts are severed, it seems to last an eternity.'"

When the feuding royal couple heard this their enmity immediately disappeared, and they became as one for the rest of their days.[31]

The queen of the chief king of India had failed to produce an heir, and his subjects complained that the realm would perish if there was no successor to the throne. It was suggested that the king adopt a child thus: "Send out a band of women, decreeing it a religious duty for the males of your kingdom to have intercourse with them. Surely at least one of the women will conceive a child."

None of the women did, however, nor was there any success with a second and third band of potential surrogate mothers. Finally it was decided to offer the queen herself. A long queue formed the day this peerless beauty was put up for grabs. The god Sakka, determined to grant the good king and queen their wish, disguised himself as a randy old man and used his magical powers to place himself at the head of the line.

"What are you doing here, you old fool?" the others jeered.

"I may be old, but I still love sex and I want to have my jollies with the queen," said Sakka, as he acted the part of a lecher. Mesmerized by the god's powers, the queen went off with him, much to everyone's amazement and the king's great dismay.

After causing her to lose consciousness with the "thrill of his divine touch," Sakka escorted the queen to the Heaven of the Thirty-Three. The queen awoke, and Sakka informed her of his intention to grant her not one but two sons: "One, however, will be wise but ugly; the other will be handsome but a fool. Which one do you want to bear first?"

"The wise one," answered the queen.

"Good," said Sakka. He then transported her back to the king's bedchamber. (It required much proof to convince the king that his wife had actually been to heaven and not simply off somewhere fornicating with the old man.) As promised, she conceived and a son was born. He was named Kusa. About a year later the second son appeared, and he was called Jayampati.

When Kusa was sixteen years old, his father turned the throne over to him. The king added that the time had come for the young man to select a queen. Kusa initially refused, saying that he was thinking of becoming a monk, and, besides, no woman would want to marry him because he was so ugly. His parents were adamant, though, and Kusa concocted the following plan to avoid marriage: He had a golden statue made of a celestial nymph, and then said to his mother, confident that no such being existed on this earth, "Find me a maiden as lovely as this, and she will be my queen."

Following a long search, the queen mother's emissaries were able to locate a girl fairer than the angels. The radiant princess, known as Pabhāvatī, was brought back to the palace. When the queen mother saw Pabhāvatī, she at once realized, "She is indeed beautiful, and she won't want to spend a minute with our ugly son. I must devise a scheme."

"In our kingdom," the queen mother told the princess and her father, "We have a custom. A wife is not allowed to observe her husband in daylight until she has conceived." Pabhāvatī and her father agreed to that stipulation, and she and Kusa were wed late that night.

The couple had access to each other in the dark but never laid eyes on each other during the day. Kusa longed for a glimpse of his fair queen out in the open; so the queen mother had him dress as servant so he could catch occasional glimpses of Pabhāvatī. Kusa, unfortunately, could not control himself when he saw her and kept trying to attract her attention, eventually making a nuisance of himself. When Pabhāvatī demanded to see her husband in broad daylight, the queen mother substituted Jayampati, Kusa's handsome brother, at the head of a procession safely out of Pabhāvatī's reach.

The charade could not continue forever, and finally the truth came out. Pabhāvatī fell into a faint at the sight of Kusa's misshapen features and fled back to her father's kingdom. Kusa was devastated. Determined to win back his queen at any cost, he set out after her. Upon reaching the kingdom of Pabhāvatī's father, Kusa disguised himself, secured a position in the palace as a cook, and was able to meet Pabhāvatī.

Stunned, she demanded that he leave immediately, crying, "I can't stand the sight of you!"

Kusa pleaded with her to come back. "It is you and only you that I love. If you are not my queen, my throne is worthless." Kusa pretended to swoon, hoping to elicit a more gentle response from Pabhāvatī. She knelt briefly by his side, but when she realized that he was merely pretending she cursed him and ran away.

Kusa continued to be smitten with Pabhāvatī, but her heart was very hard. Once one of Pabhāvatī's servants, appalled at the scorn the queen was heaping on Kusa, lashed out, "Beauty is only skin deep. Kusa may not be pleasant to look at, but consider his other virtues—he is wealthy, powerful, master of a hundred arts, and a great warrior." Pabhāvatī nevertheless remained totally aloof, and after seven fruitless months Kusa was ready to give up his quest to win her heart.

When other princes learned that Pabhāvatī had thrown over the chief king of India, they rushed to the palace to seek her hand in marriage. Fighting broke out among them, and they threatened to storm the palace; whoever got to Pabhāvatī first could have her. In order to save his realm the king proposed sacrificing his daughter by having her body cut up into seven pieces, one for each of the feuding princes. Her mother cried out in anguish, "If only King Kusa were here to protect his queen."

Pabhāvatī informed her parents that Kusa was in fact in the palace. He had been working as a cook, trying to win her love. Following a lengthy series of apologies—including a scene in which

Pabhāvatī begs for forgiveness while wallowing in mud Kusa prepared especially for the occasion—Kusa reassumes his position as Pabhāvatī's king and crushes the invading armies. This Buddhist version of "The Beauty and the Beast" concludes: "Kusa and Pabhāvatī were henceforth truly man and wife, dwelling forever in peace and love."[32]

There is also a Buddhist version of "The Frog Prince." In the Buddhist fable, the prince is a princess so hideous that her father had to keep her hidden away. The only one who would marry her was a former nobleman who had fallen on hard times and was reduced to living as a beggar: "Even if you gave me a bitch from your kennels, I would accept it as my wife." Following the marriage, the girl began contemplating Buddha's glorious form, concentrating on different attributes each time. As she visualized each section of Buddha's body, her own form acquired similar qualities. Eventually she became exquisitely beautiful, and she and her husband lived happily ever after.[33]

It is a widely held belief in the East that couples deeply in love have been partners in their previous lives as well. This was certainly thought so of Gotama and Yaśodharā, who were said to have been paired in a variety of previous human and animal incarnations.[34] In Japan, the notion of perpetual union was very strong. A popular Japanese folk song contains this verse:

> Love has nothing to do with reason;
> Our love-knot was tied long ago in a former life.

Japanese women often became nuns upon the death of their husbands and lovers, vowing to remain chaste until they joined their partners again in the next world.

Then there is the tale from Buddhist Korea of a young pleasure girl who captivated an older gentleman who doted on her. He was called away on official duty but promised to make her his second wife upon his return. When he did not come back, the girl set out to search for him. One night she was stranded in the mountains by a blizzard. She found refuge in what appeared to be an empty hut and fell asleep exhausted. During the night, the occupant of the hermitage, a young monk, became inflamed with passion and raped her.

The monk had faithfully observed the precepts until that time

135

and was remorseful the following morning. They were snowed in for the winter, however, and making the best of a seemingly bad situation the two decided to live in harmony. After a time they grew more intimate, and the monk said to the girl, "It was karmic affinity that brought us together. Why not grow old together, sharing a peaceful and happy life?" The girl agreed, and they married, prospered, and had many children and grandchildren.[35]

There is this bizarre tale which could be called "The Fat Woman Who Knew How to Shit." After Buddha and several of his monks visited a certain king, the monks asked Buddha why the king had taken such a fat woman for his queen. Buddha replied, "Long ago, a corpulent peasant woman passed by the king's palace. Nature called, and she relieved herself by the side of the road. The king just happened to be looking out the window then and was taken with the dignity and grace with which the woman handled the emergency. Thinking to himself, 'If she acts like that even in private, she must be a good and decent woman.' The king took her as his queen, and she did turn out to be an excellent wife and mother, giving birth to a son who eventually became a universal monarch. In this present life, the king and his fat queen have been reunited."[36]

What are the sexual ethics of Buddhism?

Throughout the Buddhist world a set of precepts, somewhat similar to the Ten Commandments of the Bible, are widely observed, at least in principle. One of those precepts is "To refrain from sexual misconduct."[37] In puritan Buddhism this is interpreted very narrowly for monks and nuns: no sexual activity of any kind, for any reason.

Non-monastic Buddhists made the same pledge. Presumably this meant that single men and women should be celibate, but in actual practice parents married off their children at such early ages in the East that the problem of "premarital" sex never became much of an issue. Since marriage or sexual bonds to more than one person was an option for Buddhists (in some cultures), chastity for mature males basically consisted of avoiding sex with the following kinds of women: minors, close relatives, girls under the protection of their parents, betrothed girls, women married to other men, adulterous women, female convicts, and, of course, nuns.[38] While not stated explicitly, a similar unwritten code was in force for women. An interesting feature of Buddhism is that courtesans are recorded as faithfully observing all the precepts—and one, as we have seen in chapter 3, was even the heroine of a sutra. Evidently, because their occupation was an accepted one, their professional behavior was not classified as sexual misconduct, and one Buddhist courtesan is even praised as "always giving the customer his money's worth."[39] Although there may have been superstitious or cultural reasons for avoiding certain kinds of sexual behavior in some Buddhist communities, there are no formal prohibitions against sex acts conducted between consenting, nonmonastic, heterosexual adult couples (or, for that matter, between humans and cooperative animals).[40] There is, however, a special Buddhist hell reserved for adulterers, rapists, pederasts, and other sex criminals.[41]

Unlike other world religions that possess elaborate theologies of marriage, Buddhism has very little to say about the subject, considering marriage (and divorce) a matter of secular concern. This is in keeping with the earliest traditions. Buddha is mentioned as having attended wedding ceremonies, but only as a guest, never a priest who sanctifies the union.[42] In some areas Buddhist priests may bless the newlyweds, but in other places—Tibet, for example—the mere presence of a Buddhist priest at a wedding ceremony is thought to bring bad luck.[43] In old Japan, most Buddhist couples preferred to take their marriage vows at Shinto shrines.

A few texts list the types of wives that a man may have: murderous, deceitful, domineering, motherly, sisterly, friendly, and, best of all, subservient. The first three types are evil women doomed to perdition. The second four are a good find.[44] Wives bring five strengths to a marriage: (sexual) attractiveness, wealth, virtue, vigor, and the ability to bear children. All these, however, can be negated by one strength of the husband—authority. (Hence the five woes of a female: having to leave home at a tender age, menstruation, pregnancy, childbirth, and having to wait on a man.)[45]

Sometimes monogamy is recommended. One of the chief attributes of a Buddhist man, one text states, is "to be content with just one wife" (with the stipulation that he is not subject to her will).[46] On the other hand, when Buddha was asked by a father, "I

137

have four daughters with four suitors. They asked me to pair them. One of the suitors is a distinguished older man, one is very handsome, one is virtuous, and one is of noble birth. What should I do?"

"Give all four to the virtuous suitor," Buddha instructed. "A virtuous man is always the best kind of husband and he will make your daughters happy." [47]

Another text briefly outlines the duties of an exemplary Buddhist couple. The husband should give his wife courtesy and respect, be faithful to her, share authority, and provide her with all things pleasing to a woman. [48] The wife, for her part, should be the first to rise in the morning and the last to retire at night. She should possess a sweet and gentle manner and be a tireless homemaker, a careful manager of the household finances, and a charming hostess. [49] This traditional patriarchal view of marriage, found the world over, is of course not an essential part of Buddhism.

Divorce is rarely mentioned in Buddhist literature. One layman in Buddha's time decided to embrace celibacy and relinquished his marriage vows to his four wives. When he asked them what they wanted in terms of a settlement, one said, "Give me to Mr. So-and-so!" The man was summoned, and the first husband performed a simple ceremony to bind the new couple together. [50] There is an example of a young wife leaving her philandering husband to become a nun. Even though he completely ignored her while they were married, the husband one day realized what he had lost and wanted her back. "Sorry," she told him. "I'm perfectly happy the way I am." [51] In Japan there was a Buddhist temple called Tokei-ji where abused wives could seek shelter from their brutish husbands. The women were given sanctuary for three years, serving as lay nuns, and then they could obtain a legal divorce.

There is a reference to a married woman committing adultery in her heart—she had lustful designs on a king who drove by in procession—but when she confessed to her Buddhist elders, they assured her that thoughts do not constitute a sin. (Nevertheless, she still felt that she had tarnished her virtue.) [52]

Before taking up the questions of birth control and abortion, we need to consider Buddhist embryology and the belief that every child is a potential Buddha. [53]

Ideally, at the moment of conception both the mother and the father are senseless with bliss, melting together to create a psychophysical mandala. If conditions are right, the white drop (sperm) of the father will unite with the red drop (ovum) of the mother. This point of union will later develop into the child's heart. From the white drop, the fetus will develop sperm, marrow, and bones; from the red drop, internal organs, blood, flesh, and skin. A fetus contains both male and female elements (a finding confirmed by modern science),[54] and its sex is not clearly defined until the eleventh or twelfth week. The fetus is attracted to one or the other parent; if it is repelled by the mother and attracted to the father, it will be a female child; if the opposite occurs, it will be a male. The fetus is complete by the twenty-eighth week; in the thirty-sixth week it begins to develop a strong dislike for the darkness and dirtiness of the womb and begins to want to emerge. The feeling intensifies until the thirty-eighth week, and then the child is born.[55]

Since birth control could be interpreted as an attempt to interfere with the workings of karma, there was a tendency in Buddhism to discourage artificial contraception. In reality, however, the necessity of birth control was tacitly recognized, and a contraception was controlled in a variety of ways—abstention from sex (the rhythm method), control of the male's ejaculation, and, from the time of Buddha, birth control pills.[56]

Abortion, however, was an abomination. In addition to being a violation of the precept against killing a living being, it was destruction of a potential Buddha and a crime against the maintenance of the human race.[57] Mitigating factors such as impregnation by rape or incest may have been considered, but the Buddhist position against abortion was clearcut and has only been questioned in modern times.

Equally controversial, past and present, is the problem and nature of homosexuality, perhaps the only sex act condemned by both the puritan and Tantric Buddhists.[58] Although it may have been officially proscribed, homosexuality in fact flourished in Buddhist monasteries throughout the centuries: In China the character for hemorrhoids is "temple illness"; male love is said to not have existed in Japan until it was introduced by Buddhist monks in the ninth century;[59] homosexuality was prevalent in Yellow Hat mon-

139

asteries in Tibet and was regarded as a virtue, since it meant that a monk had completely conquered sexual attachment to women;[60] even today in Korean monasteries a young trainee must "watch his ass" at all times.[61] Whether or not the existence of homosexuality constitutes its acceptance as a sexual orientation in Buddhism is another thorny question. The complex issues of abortion and homosexuality in Buddhism require a separate forum, and a more detailed evaluation must wait for another occasion.

Buddhist sexual ethics are both situational and absolute. Each sexual encounter is unique, with a special network of contributing factors. It is the motive, not the act itself, which must be ethical.

In sharp contrast to Judaism, Christianity, and Islam, in which sexual relations are regulated in detail, Buddhist moralists focused on the essentials. Jiun, a monk who was a master of both Shingon and Zen Buddhism, was renowned for his strict observance of the precepts. Yet his commentary on the pledge "To refrain from sexual misconduct" is anything but a prudish harping on what human beings can and cannot do when they make love:

> Look for liberation in the midst of the realm of samsara. As the Zen Master Rinzai [Lin-chi] stated, "Cling to the sacred and disdain the profane and you will be sunk in the ocean of life and death forever." Since male and female elements exist, they must possess virtue. Because there are men and women, passion naturally exists. It is foolish to say that passion is "nothing." Passion is a useful tool for attaining enlightenment. Realize this and all your actions will be stainless. Men and women belong together; together they can proceed on the true Path. This is the meaning of "To refrain from sexual misconduct."[62]

If the act of sex is consummated selflessly and with compassion, if it is mutually enriching and ennobling, if it deepens one's understanding of Buddhism, promotes integration and spiritual emancipation, and is, above all, beneficial to *all* the parties involved, it is "good." If, on the contrary, sex erupts from animal passion, is based purely on physical pleasure, and originates in the desire to possess, dominate, or degrade, it is "evil."

The one absolute standard is that no one involved be harmed or deceived in any way. "In certain cases, a Bodhisattva, relying on skillful means, may destroy life, take what is not given, commit sexual misconduct, and drink intoxicants, but a Bodhisattva must never lie or deceive others, for that violates the reality of things." [63] Whenever there is a sex scandal in a Buddhist community—and there have been many over the centuries—the primary cause of the trouble is sure to be deceit: people deceiving their disciples, families, and friends, deceiving their communities, and lying to themselves.

Regarding the ethics of sex, love, and marriage, good Buddhists have always relied on this essential moral standard:

If your heart is pure, all things in your world will be pure.

When this is true, even lust may win us enlightenment.

141

Notes

CHAPTER 1. THE SEX LIFE OF THE BUDDHA

1. Material in this chapter is a composite drawn from the following sources.

Pali texts: I. B. Horner, *The Collection of Middle Length Sayings*, 3 vols. (London: Pali Text Society, 1979); C. A. F. Rhys Davids and F. L. Woodward, *The Book of Kindred Sayings*, 5 vols. (London: Pali Text Society, 1979); T. W. Rhys Davids and C. A. F. Rhys Davids, *Dialogues of the Buddha*, 3 vols. (London: Pali Text Society, 1977); F. L. Woodward and E. M. Hare, *The Book of Gradual Sayings*, 5 vols. (London: Pali Text Society, 1979); I. B. Horner, *Book of the Discipline*, 6 vols. (London: Pali Text Society, 1982); T. W. Rhys Davids and H. Oldenberg, *Vinaya Texts*, 3 vols. (Delhi: Motilal Banarsidass, 1968 reprint); and E. W. Burlingame, *Buddhist Legends*, 3 vols. (London: Pali Text Society, 1969).

Classical biographies of the Buddha: G. Bays, *The Voice of the Buddha: Lalitavistara Sutra*, 2 vols. (Berkeley: Dharma Publishing, 1983); S. Beal, *Fo-Sho-Hing-Tsan-King: A Life of Buddha* (Delhi: Motilal Banarsidass, reprint 1968); S. Beal, *The Romantic Legend of Śākya Buddha* (Delhi: Motilal Banarsidass, reprint, 1985); E. H. Johnston, *The Buddhacarita or Acts of the Buddha* (Delhi: Motilal Banarsidass, 1984); J. J. Jones, *The Mahāvastu*, 3 vols. (London: Pali Text Society, 1973); N. Poppe, *The Twelve Deeds of Buddha* (Wiesbaden: Otto Harrassowitz, 1967); and W. W. Rockwell, *The Life of Buddha* (London: Trubner's Oriental Series, 1884).

Pictorial biographies: J. Auboyer et al., *Buddha: A Pictorial History of His Life and Legacy* (New Delhi: Roli Books International, 1983); and N. J. Krom, *The Life of Buddha on the Stupa of Barabudur* (Delhi: Bhartiya Publishing House, 1974).

Modern biographies: A. Coomaraswamy, *Buddha and the Gospel of Buddhism* (Secaucus, N.J.: Citadel Press, 1988); A. Foucher, *The Life of Buddha* (Westport, Conn.: Greenwood Press, 1963); P. Herbert, *The Life of the Buddha* (London: British Museum, 1990). D. J. Kalupahana

Notes

and I. Kalupahana, *The Way of Siddhartha: A Life of the Buddha* (Boulder: Shambhala Publications, 1983); A. Lillie, *The Life of Buddha* (Delhi: Seema Publications, 1974); Nanamoli, *The Life of the Buddha* (Kandy: Buddhist Publication Society, 1972); H. Nakamura, *Gotama Buddha* (Los Angeles & Tokyo: Buddhist Books International, 1977); and E. J. Thomas, *The Life of Buddha as Legend and History* (London: Routledge & Kegan Paul, reprint 1969). There is also a novel on the subject by W. E. Barrett, *Lady of the Lotus: The Untold Love Story of The Buddha and His Wife* (Los Angeles: Jeremy P. Tarcher, 1975).

2. See, for example, Bays, *Voice of the Buddha,* vol. 1, p. 42; Beal, *Romantic Legend*, p. 32; and Thomas, *Life of Buddha*, p. 29.

3. Bays, *Voice of the Buddha*, vol. 1., pp. 44–45, and Jones, *Mahāvastu*, vol. 2, pp. 7ff.

4. The *Mahāvastu* states that the Buddha deliberately incarnates himself into the womb of a woman who has only ten months and seven days to live because it would not be proper for her to "indulge in the pleasures of love after giving birth to a Peerless One" (vol. 2, p. 3).

5. This description of Gotama is based on the thirty-two distinguishing marks of a Buddha. See Bays, *Voice of the Buddha*, vol. 1, pp. 155ff.; Beal, *Romantic History*, p. 55; Rhys Davids and Rhys Davids, *Dialogues of the Buddha*, vol. 3, pp. 138ff.; Jones, *Mahāvastu*, vol. 1, pp. 180–181; and Thomas, *Life of Buddha*, pp. 220–221, which lists both the thirty-two major and eighty minor characteristics of a Buddha. For further information on Buddha's physical form, see. D. L. Snellgrove, ed., *The Image of the Buddha* (Tokyo: Kodansha International, 1978).

6. The Chinese texts (e.g., Beal, *Fo-Sho-Hing-Tsan-King*, p. 14) state that Buddha's sex organs were hidden like those of a stallion. According to the Tibetan tradition, the Dalai Lamas are supposed to possess a similar ability to "retract" their sex organs; see M. Aris, *Hidden Treasures and Secret Lives* (Delhi: Motilal Banarsidass, 1988), p. 197.

7. In Buddha's time, there were "public days" in which unmarried girls, who were normally sequestered, would promenade through the town in hopes of capturing the fancy of a young man. See H. C. Warren, *Buddhism in Translation* (Cambridge: Harvard University Press, 1986), p. 455.

8. Jones, *Mahāvastu*, vol. 2, p. 70, and Krom, plate 48.

9. Beal, *Romantic Legend*, p. 92. Plate 19 in W. Zwalf, *Buddhism: Art and Faith* (London: British Museum Publications, 1985), seems to depict a wedding scene of Gotama and one of his wives.

10. Bays, *Voice of the Buddha*, vol. 1, pp. 235–236, and Krom, plate 55.

11. Thomas, *Life of Buddha*, pp. 48ff., discusses the different names given Buddha's wives.

144

12. Beal, *Romantic Legend*, pp. 96ff.
13. This exchange occurs in T. Cleary, *The Flower Ornament Scripture* (Boston: Shambhala Publications, 1987), pp. 284–288.
14. For examples of lush Buddhist beauties see S. Huntington and J. Huntington, *The Art of Ancient India* (Tokyo: John Weatherhill, 1987); G. Michael et al., *In the Image of Man* (London: Weidenfeld & Nicolson, 1982); P. Rawson, *Erotic Art of the East* (New York: G. P. Putnam's Sons, 1968); and *Oriental Erotic Art* (London: Quartet Books, 1987).
15. Auboyer, *Buddha*, plates 16, 19–21, and 94, illustrates Gotama's life of pleasure in the palace. For descriptions and illustrations of the love life of an Indian prince, see P. K. Agrawal, *Mithuna* (New Delhi: Munshiram Manoharal, 1983); H. Bach, *Indian Love Paintings* (New Delhi: Lustre Press, 1985); R. Burton, *The Illustrated Kama Sutra* (Middlesex: Hamlyn, 1987); N. Douglas and P. Singer, *The Pillow Book* (New York: Destiny Books, 1984) and *Sexual Secrets* (New York: Destiny Books, 1986); S. N. Prasad, *Kalyāṇamalla's Anaṅgaraṅga* (New Delhi: Chaukhambha Orientalia, 1983); and E. Windsor, *The Hindu Art of Love* (New York: Panurge Press, 1932).
16. Beal, *Romantic Legend*, p. 101.
17. Johnston, *Buddhacarita*, p. 26.
18. See Rawson's description of the sex life of an Indian prince in classical times, *Erotic Art of the East*, p. 65.
19. J. Campbell, *The Masks of God: Oriental Mythology* (London: Penguin Books, 1973), p. 259.
20. Bays, *Voice of the Buddha*, vol. 1 pp. 291 and 304ff.; Beal, *Romantic Legend*, p. 123; and Krom, *Life of Buddha*, plate 65.
21. Johnston, *Buddhacarita*, pp. 44ff.
22. Ibid., p. 53.
23. Beal, *Romantic Legend*, p. 128. The Chinese text was so explicit that Beal did not translate it.
24. Poppe, *Twelve Deeds*, p. 118.
25. Bays, *Voice of the Buddha*, vol. 1, pp. 310ff.; Beal, *Fo-Sho-Hing-Tsan-King*, p. 54; Beal, *Romantic Legend*, pp. 130ff.; Foucher, pp. 73ff.; Jones, *Mahāvastu*, vol. 2, pp. 70ff.; and Krom, *Life of the Buddha*, plates 68 and 69. "Disgust with the dancing girls" also plays a role in the story of Yasa, an early convert to Buddhism. See Rhys Davids and Oldenberg, *Vinaya Texts*, vol. 1, pp. 102ff.
26. See Beal, *Romantic Legend*, p. 130.
27. Poppe, *Twelve Deeds*, p. 124.
28. For a picture of this scene, see H. Bechert and R. Gombrich, *Buddhism* (London: Thames and Hudson, 1984), p. 21, plate 10.

29. See Johnston, *Buddhacarita*, p. 116.
30. See Lillie, *Life of Buddha*, pp. 66–67.
31. In Poppe, *Twelve Deeds*, p. 123, Buddha says: "There is not a single sensual joy which I have not enjoyed." The *Buddhacarita* states that each potential Buddha must taste all sensual pleasures prior to illumination (p. 30).
32. See Bays, *Voice of the Buddha*, vol. 2, pp. 484–485.
33. Adapted after Beal, *Romantic Legend*, p. 211–212.
34. Regarding the temptation of Mara's daughters, see also Auboyer, *Buddha*, plates 52 and 56; Jones, *Mahāvastu*, vol. 3, p. 270; Krom, *The Life of the Buddha*, plate 105; and Lillie, *Life of Buddha*, pp. 91–92. Young boys are often given temporary ordination in the Theravadan countries of Southeast Asia, and the "Temptation of Mara's Daughters" is re-enacted during the ceremony. See R. C. Lester, *Theravada Buddhism in Southeast Asia* (Ann Arbor: University of Michigan Press, 1973), pp. 91–92.
35. Beal, *Romantic Legend*, p. 226.
36. Thomas, *Life of Buddha*, p. 79.
37. Bays, *Voice of the Buddha*, vol. 2, p. 649.
38. Ibid., p. 572.
39. Coomaraswamy, *Buddha and the Gospel of Buddhism*, p. 49.
40. After Gotama's departure from the palace, Yaśodharā's mood remained "dull and dark" (Beal, *Romantic Legend*, p. 92). As mentioned in the text, it is also recorded that when Yaśodharā first met her former husband she tried to win him back by wearing her most alluring clothes and feeding him sweetmeats (Jones, *Mahāvastu*, vol. 2, p. 260). In the *Romantic Legend* it says that Buddha's son was born six years *after* he had left the palace. Naturally, Yaśodharā was suspected of infidelity and the text lamely tries to explain away her supposed six-year pregnancy as the result of bad karma accumulated in a previous life (pp. 360ff.). In the *Apadāna* it reports that Yaśodharā told Buddha when she met him late in life that she had been her own refuge and had done quite well on her own account. See I. B. Horner, *Woman in Primitive Buddhism* (Delhi: Motilal Banarsidass, 1975), p. 310.

Chapter 2. Extinguish the Flames

1. Rhys Davids and Woodward, *Kindred Sayings*, vol. 4, p. 10.
2. Cf. D. Paul, *Woman in Buddhism* (Berkeley: Asian Humanities Press, 1979), pp. 44ff.

3. D. Goddard, *A Buddhist Bible* (Boston: Beacon Press, 1966), p. 263.
4. Rhys Davids and Oldenberg, *Vinaya Texts*, vol. 1, p. 116.
5. Woodward and Hare, *Gradual Sayings*, vol. 1, pp. 1–2.
6. Burlingame, *Buddhist Legends*, vol. 2, p. 218.
7. D. Snellgrove, *Indo-Tibetan Buddhism*, vol. 1 (Boston: Shambhala Publications, 1987), p. 86.
8. Horner, *Middle Length Sayings*, vol. 1, p. 369.
9. Beal, *Romantic Legend*, p. 216.
10. Poppe, *Twelve Deeds*, p. 122.
11. See E. Conze, *Buddhist Meditation* (New York; Harper & Row, 1956), pp. 103ff.; Khantipalo, *Bag of Bones* (Kandy: Buddhist Publication Society, 1980); and *The Path of Freedom: Vimittimagga* (Kandy: Buddhist Publication Society, 1977), pp. 132ff. *Buddhist Legends*, vol. 1, p. 206, describes the contemplation of a corpse of a pregnant woman.
12. Burlingame, *Buddhist Legends*, vol. 2, pp. 331ff.
13. See Y. S. Hakeda, *Kūkai: Major Works* (New York: Columbia University Press, 1972), p. 131.
14. Burlingame, *Buddhist Legends*, vol. 2, pp. 336ff. For a similar tale from the Chinese canon see Lillie, pp. 288ff.
15. S. Frye, *Sūtra of the Wise and the Foolish* (Dharamsala: Library of Tibetan Works & Archives, 1981), pp. 232ff. Also Lillie, pp. 323ff.
16. Ibid., p. 233.
17. Khantipalo, *Bag of Bones*, p. 20.
18. It seems that such extreme emphasis on the foulness of the body actually backfired. Buddha recommended this meditation practice to his monks, but when he returned he wondered why so many of his followers had disappeared. Buddha was informed that a number of the monks had become so disgusted with their bodies that they had killed themselves. The elder Ānanda wisely suggested that Buddha come up with a different form of meditation and he did: meditation on the flow of the breath (Rhys Davids and Woodward, *Kindred Sayings*, vol. 5, pp. 284–285, and Horner, *Book of the Discipline*, vol. 1, p. 120). On another occasion, Buddha was offered the hand of a princess by a king who was ignorant of the rules of the Order. Without a bit of tact, Buddha rejected the girl with these harsh words: "I have conquered passion and have no need for sex, so why should I accept this skin-bag full of filth, something I would not even touch with my foot." The princess was understandably offended and became a sworn enemy of Buddha. She finally met a violent end but not before wreaking considerable havoc on the Order. (Burlingame, *Buddhist Legends*, vol. 1, pp. 206ff.)

19. See E. H. Johnston, *The Saundarananda of Aśvoghoṣa* (Delhi: Motilal Banarsidass, 1988 reprint).
20. *Bodhi Leaves*, no. B 106 (Kandy: Buddhist Publication Society, 1985), p. 10.
21. E. B. Cowell, ed., *Jātaka or Stories of the Buddha's Former Births*, 3 vols. (London: Pali Text Society, 1981). This is Jātaka no. 527. (Since there are so many different editions of the Jātaka reference will be made to the story number rather than the page number.) See also J. Jones's excellent book *The Tales and Teachings of the Buddha* (London: George Allen & Unwin, 1979).
22. Jātakas 66, 251, and 431.
23. Jātaka 425. Half of the gold went directly to the courtesan and half went to keep her in fine clothes, perfumes, and garlands.
24. Jātakas 523 and 526.
25. Jātaka 207.
26. Burlingame, *Buddhist Legends*, vol. 3, pp. 340ff.
27. Ibid., p. 85.
28. Rhys Davids and Oldenberg, *Vinaya Texts*, vol. 3, p. 289.
29. Jātaka 273. This was originally put into Latin, not English, by the translator.
30. Jātaka 106.
31. See Horner, *Woman in Primitive Buddhism*, and S. E. Jootla, *Inspiration from Enlightened Nuns* (Kandy: Buddhist Publication Society, 1988).
32. Frye, *Sūtra of the Wise and the Foolish*, pp. 128ff.
33. Jātaka 408.
34. H. Hecker, *Mahā Kassapa* (Kandy: Buddhist Publication Society, 1988), pp. 3ff.
35. Horner, *Book of the Discipline*, vol. 1, pp. 32ff.
36. Rhys Davids and Oldenberg, *Vinaya Texts*, vol. 1, p. 235. In puritan Buddhism, ordination is supposed to mark the birth of an asexual being (Lester, p. 86).
37. As noted above, the *Vinaya* has been translated into English, but some of it was just too much for the Victorian attitudes of the translators. Much of what appears here, likely for the first time in English, was either bowdlerized or omitted altogether from those translations.
38. Horner, *Book of the Discipline*, vol. 1, pp. 38ff. Monks were also reported misbehaving with cows (Rhys Davids and Oldenberg, *Vinaya Texts*, vol. 2, p. 24).
39. Horner, *Book of the Discipline*, vol. 1, pp. 40ff.
40. Ibid., pp. 47ff.
41. Ibid., pp. 55ff.

42. Ibid., p. 58.
43. Ibid., p. 61.
44. Ibid., p. 53.
45. Ibid., pp. 53ff.
46. Ibid., pp. 60ff.
47. Ibid., p. 113.
48. Ibid., pp. 144ff.
49. Ibid., p. 123.
50. Ibid., p. 144.
51. Ibid., pp. 192ff.
52. Ibid., pp. 195ff. Most of this information was omitted in Horner's translation.
53. Ibid., pp. 199ff.
54. Ibid., p. 214ff.
55. Ibid., p. 220.
56. Ibid., pp. 222ff.
57. Ibid., pp. 230ff.
58. Ibid., pp. 234ff.
59. Ibid., pp. 330ff.
60. Ibid., pp. 280ff.
61. Ibid., vol. 2, pp. 30ff.
62. Ibid., pp. 37ff.
63. Ibid., pp. 198ff.
64. Burlingame, *Buddhist Legends*, vol. 3, pp. 308ff.
65. The monk had reason to worry. There was a case of a woman who, when rebuffed by a monk, scratched herself all over in order to frame him for rape. This incident resulted in the rule "All monks must keep their fingernails cut short." (Rhys Davids and Oldenberg, *Vinaya Texts*, vol. 3, p. 136.)
66. Frye, *Sūtra of the Wise and the Foolish*, pp. 81ff.
67. P. Thera, *The Virgin's Eye* (Kandy: Buddhist Publication Society, 1980), pp. 22ff.
68. S. Ōta, *Sei Sūhai* (Tokyo: Reimei Shobō, 1986), pp. 333ff.
69. Rhys Davids and Oldenberg, *Vinaya Texts*, vol. 3, p. 335.
70. See Hare, *Gradual Sayings*, vol. 4, pp. 182ff.; Rhys Davids and Oldenberg, *Vinaya Texts*, vol. 3, pp. 320ff. Most of the original nuns were widows or abandoned wives, a tendency that has continued through the centuries. The majority of Buddhist nuns in the West are either widows or divorcees. Virgin nuns in the West are rare, if not nonexistent. See, for example, L. Friedman, *Meetings with Remarkable Women* (Boston: Shambhala Publications, 1987), and K. L. Tsomo,

Sakyadhītā, Daughters of the Buddha (Ithaca, N.Y.: Snow Lion: 1988).

71. See A. Hirakawa, *Monastic Discipline for the Buddhist Nuns* (Patna: Kashi Prasad Jayaswal Research Institute, 1982).

72. Rhys Davids and Oldenberg, *Vinaya Texts*, vol. 3, p. 364.

73. Hirakawa, *Monastic Discipline*, pp. 103ff and 111ff.

74. Rhys Davids and Oldenberg, *Vinaya Texts*, vol. 2, p. 222.

75. Hirakawa, *Monastic Discipline*, pp. 254ff.

76. Ibid., p. 392ff.

77. Ibid., pp. 103 and 385.

78. Rhys Davids and Oldenberg, *Vinaya Texts*, vol. 3, p. 346. This section was not translated in the English edition.

79. Khantipalo, *Bag of Bones*, pp. 5ff.

80. Rāhula, Gotama's son, was given similar advice: "Regard all women as your mother—gracious, sweet, beautiful, and chaste (Jones, *Mahāvastu*, vol. 2, p. 254).

81. Rhys Davids and Rhys Davids, *Dialogues of the Buddha*, vol. 2, p. 154.

82. Warren, *Buddhism in Translation*, p. 297.

83. Bechert and Gombrich, p. 31.

84. Burlingame, *Buddhist Legends*, vol. 1, p. 217.

85. Ibid., vol. 3, pp. 290–291. This question came up following the rape of the nun Uppalavanna. Evidently, the position of some of Buddha's disciples was that since the nun was spiritually advanced and without sinful thoughts, she should have "relaxed and enjoyed it." Human beings are not made of stone so why shouldn't an arhat, they wanted to know, have sex like everyone else? Buddha's reply is a bit ambiguous and could be taken to mean that sex may be performed if done so on a higher level. This interpretation was rejected by the puritans, and there are references in the canon warning monks and nuns to be wary of those Buddhists who maintained that sex is no obstacle to proper religious practice (Hirakawa, *Monastic Discipline*, p. 238).

86. These are the seven bonds of sex to be avoided by monks (Woodward and Hare, *Gradual Sayings,* vol. 4, pp. 31–32).

87. V. Mackenzie, *Reincarnation: The Boy Lama* (London: Bloomsbury, 1988), p. 160.

88. For a sympathetic treatment of monastic celibacy in Buddhism, see K. Inwood, Bhikku, *Disciple of the Buddha* (Bangkok: Thai Watona Danich, 1981).

89. Goddard, *A Buddhist Bible*, p. 112.

90. See Goddard, *A Buddhist Bible*, p. 110. Ānanda is rescued by Mañjuśrī at the last minute from the arms of an enticing beauty who had cast a spell on him. In another text, Ānanda is saved by Buddha himself just

as he is about to succumb to a voluptuous outcaste maid (Thera, *The Virgin's Eye*, pp. 16ff.). Āṇanda is also reported to have made this puzzling statement: "I know that women are full of passion, but I thought if they would see the private parts of the Buddha's Body, they would be liberated from their sexuality" (E. Obermiller, *Buston: History of Buddhism* [Heidelberg: privately published, 1932], vol. 1, p. 80).

91. Woodward and Hare, *Gradual Sayings*, vol. 1, p. 148ff. Āṇanda cures a nun of her passion for him with a discourse on the loathsomeness of the body; sexual intercourse, he cautions her, breaks down the bridge to liberation.

92. Rhys Davids and Oldenberg, *Vinaya Texts*, vol. 3, p. 77. Buddha said, "That monk should have cut off his disturbing thoughts instead of his member."

93. Horner, *Women in Primitive Buddhism*, p. 183.

94. M. E. Spiro, *Buddhism and Society* (New York: Harper & Row, 1963), p. 367.

95. Tsomo, *Sakyadhītā*, p. 298.

96. A typical example is *Monks and Nuns in a Sea of Sins*, translated from the Chinese by H. S. Levy (Taipei: The Chinese Association for Folklore, 1975). See also L. Siegel, *Laughing Matters* (Chicago: University of Chicago Press, 1987), p. 210ff., for satire in Sanskrit literature on bogus Buddhist monks. One such monk recites this poem: "So many times I've embraced buxom sluts with passion, / wrapping strong arms around 'em in ardent fashion; / But by all Buddhas I'll swear a hundred times, I will, / That never have I experienced so great a thrill / As when I held this yogi's girl in close, fervent hugs, / My delighting hands upon her firm and swelling jugs" (p. 213).

97. H. S. Levy, *Japanese Sex Jokes in Traditional Times* (Washington, D.C.: Warm-Soft Press, 1973), p. 121.

98. H. S. Levy, *Chinese Sex Jokes in Traditional Times* (Washington, D.C.: Warm-Soft Press, 1973), p. 230.

99. Spiro, *Buddhism and Society*, p. 367.

100. J. Bunnag, *Buddhist Monk, Buddhist Layman* (Cambridge: Cambridge University Press, 1973), pp. 190, 193.

101. Burlingame, *Buddhist Legends*, vol. 3, pp. 24ff. Unfortunately, the text goes on to say that while men are punished by being reborn as women, women are rewarded for good behavior by being reborn as men! The story itself is fascinating. Soreyya was changed into a woman after fathering two sons, and following his transformation he bore two more boys. He was then changed back into a man and said,

"I have experienced life from both sides, and now I would like to become a monk." When asked, "Which pair of sons do you cherish the most?" Soreyya initially replied, "The ones I bore as a woman." After becoming a monk, however, his answer changed to "I do not favor one set over the other." The biography of the Tibetan holy man Thang-stong mentions that he had been a Buddhist nun in one of his recent incarnations. J. Gyatso, "The Literary Transmission of the Traditions of Thang-stong rGyal-po" (Ph.D. thesis, University of California, Berkeley, 1981), p. 29. Although Buddha assumes nearly every other form imaginable, he almost never appears as a female incarnation in any of the birth stories.

102. Jātaka 402. In Jātaka 120, a queen makes her husband promise not to have sex with any other women in the palace, a great sacrifice on the part of the king. When he goes off to war, she asks him to send a messenger daily to inform her of his well-being. As soon as a messenger appears, however, she takes him to bed. She sleeps with sixty-four messengers in all. When the king finds out about these goings-on, he orders that everyone involved be executed. He is dissuaded from that course of action by his chief minister (a Buddha-to-be), who reasons, "The messengers were just following orders, and the queen could not help herself since women are naturally insatiable."

103. "It is impossible for a woman to become an *arhat*," Horner, *Middle Length Sayings*, vol. 3, p. 109. Since a woman lacked one of the essential marks of a Buddha—a penis and testicles—it was thought by some that this automatically disqualified her from Buddhahood. In typical Buddhist fashion, however, this claim is totally contradicted in the same part of the canon: "Countless women, both monastic and lay, have attained enlightenment" (vol. 2, pp. 169–170).

104. Y. Kajiyama, "Woman in Buddhism," *Eastern Buddhist* vol. 15, no. 2 (1982): 53–70.

105. See especially A. Bancroft, "Women in Buddhism," in *Women in the World's Religions* (New York: Paragon House, 1987), pp. 81–104; N. Barnes, "Buddhism," in *Women in World Religions* (Albany: State University of New York Press, 1987), pp. 106–133; Horner, *Women in Primitive Buddhism*; Kajiyama, "Women and Buddhism"; D. Paul, *Woman and Buddhism*; and "Woman and Buddhism," *Spring Wind* Special Issue, nos. 1–3 (1986). Incidentally, despite the misogyny of many texts, it seems that in Buddhism women were rarely considered ritually impure because of menstruation or pregancy. In Sri Lanka, for example, menstruating women may visit a Buddhist temple but are prohibited from approaching a Hindu shrine. R. Gombrich and

G. Obeyesekere, *Buddhism Transformed* (Princeton, N.J.: Princeton University Press, 1988), p. 21.
106. Jātaka 61.

CHAPTER 3. THE JEWEL IN THE LOTUS

1. Available in three English translations: E. Lamotte, *The Teaching of Vimalakīrti* (London: Pali Text Society, 1976); C. Luk, *The Vimalakīrti Nirdeśa Sūtra* (Boston: Shambhala Publications, 1990); and R. A. F. Thurman, *The Holy Teaching of Vimalakīriti* (University Park: Pennsylvania State University, 1976).
2. *Vimalakīrti Nirdeśa Sūtra*, chap. 2.
3. Ibid., chap. 3.
4. Ibid.
5. Ibid., chap. 7.
6. Ibid., chap. 8.
7. Available in two English translations: G. C. C. Chang, ed., "The True Lion's Roar of Queen Śrīmālā," *A Treasury of Mahāyāna Sūtras* (University Park: Pennsylvania State University, 1983), and A. Wayman and H. Wayman, *The Lion's Roar of Queen Śrīmālā* (New York: Columbia University Press, 1974).
8. Wayman & Wayman, *The Lion's Roar*, p. 76.
9. Ibid., pp. 78ff.
10. This has been extensively studied by K. Ku, *The Mahāyāna View of Woman: A Doctrinal Study* (Madison: University of Wisconsin, 1984). What follows is a summary of the relevant sections of her English translation of the text.
11. To the best of my knowledge this text has not been translated into English. It is text no. 149 in the *Taishō Daizōkyō*. See also Y. Iwamoto, *Bukkyō to Josei* (Tokyo: Daisan-bunmei, 1986), pp. 74ff.
12. This is text no. 818 in the *Taishō Daizōkyō*.
13. This text has been translated into English by T. Cleary and published in two editions: *The Flower Ornament Scripture*, vol. 3 (Boston: Shambhala Publications, 1987), and *Entry into the Realm of Reality: The Text* (Boston: Shambhala Publications, 1989). For an illustrated version of the tale, see J. Fontein, *The Pilgrimage of Sudhana* (The Hague: Mounton & Co., 1967).
14. Cleary, *The Flower Ornament Scripture*, vol. 3, pp. 107ff.
15. Ibid., pp. 127ff.

16. Ibid., pp. 146ff.
17. K. Ch'en, *Buddhism in China* (Princeton: Princeton University Press, 1964), p. 333.
18. D. Snellgrove, *Indo-Tibetan Buddhism*, vol. 1 (Boston: Shambhala Publications, 1988), p. 66.
19. See I. Chou, "Tantricism in China," *Harvard Journal of Asiatic Studies*, vol. 8 (1945).
20. K. Rexroth, ed., *The Buddhist Writings of Lafcadio Hearn* (London: Wildwood House, 1981), pp. 187ff.
21. D. T. Suzuki, *Essays in Zen Buddhism*, Third Series (London: Rider & Co., 1953), p. 289.
22. Ibid., p. 304.
23. See Ch'en, *Buddhism in China*, pp. 81ff., and B. N. Puri, *Buddhism in Central Asia* (Delhi: Motilal Banarsidass, 1987), pp. 116ff. In contrast, Nāgārjuna, the semilegendary master of all branches of Buddhist thought, became a monk after barely escaping execution for using his occult powers to sneak into the king's harem.
24. See M. S. Sunim, *Thousand Peaks* (Berkeley: Parallax Press, 1987), pp. 33ff.
25. See S. Arntzen, *Ikkyū and the Crazy Cloud Anthology* (Tokyo: University of Tokyo Press, 1986), p. 166.
26. See H. Hecker, "Khemā of Great Wisdom," *Buddhist Women at the Time of the Buddha* (Kandy: Buddhist Publication Society, 1985).
27. V. L. Pandit, *Woman Saints of East and West* (London: Ramakrishna Vedanta Center, 1955), p. 152.
28. Warren, *Buddhism in Translation*, pp. 451ff.
29. The best study of the Buddhist Tantra is D. Snellgrove, *Indo-Tibetan Buddhism*, 2 vols. (Boston: Shambhala Publications, 1987). See also S. B. Dasgupta, *An Introduction to Tantric Buddhism* (Calcutta: University of Calcutta, 1974); H. V. Guenther, *The Tantric View of Life* (Boulder: Shambhala Publications, 1976); and G. Tucci, *Rati-līlā* (Geneva: Nagel Publishers, 1969) and *The Theory and Practice of the Mandala* (London: Rider & Co., 1961).
30. In Buddha's time there were groups that can be clearly identified as being Tantric. In Rhys Davids and Rhys Davids, *Dialogues of the Buddha* (vol. 1, p. 49) we find mention of those who hold "the doctrine of happiness in this life and aim to attain nirvana by indulging in the pleasures to the highest degree." And many of Buddha's statements (for example, on page 46 above) can be interpreted as being Tantric. Even in puritan Buddhist texts (e.g., the *Kathāvatthu*) we find such sentiments as "breaking vows of celibacy and sexual intercourse with an-

other's wife is permissible under certain conditions of compassionate behavior." See G. S. P. Misra, *Development of Buddhist Ethics* (New Delhi: Munishiram Manoharlal, 1984), pp. 135–136.

31. See N. N. Bhattacharyya, *History of the Tantric Religion* (New Delhi: Manohar, 1987), pp. 102–103.

32. K. Dowman, *The Divine Madman* (Middletown, Calif.: Dawn Horse Press, 1980), p. 22. Reprinted by permission. See also H. V. Guenther, *The Royal Song of Sahara* (Seattle: University of Washington Press, 1969).

33. E. Bernbaum, *The Way to Shambhala* (New York: Doubleday, 1980), p. 201.

34. Both the *Hevajra* and *Guhyasamāja* Tantras open this way. The former has been translated in English by D. Snellgrove; *The Hevajra Tantra*, 2 vols. (London: Oxford University Press, 1959).

35. See Dasgupta, *Introduction to Tantric Buddhism*, pp. 102ff., and R. H. van Gulick, *Sexual Life in Ancient China* (Leiden: E. J. Brill, 1974), p. 342. It is interesting to note that the Chinese empress Wu patronized Buddhism over Taoism and Confucianism because she believed that Buddhism provided an ideological basis for the rule of the world by a woman (Chou, p. 320).

36. This and what follows is adapted from C. S. George, *The Caṇḍama-hāroṣaṇa Tantra* (New Haven, Conn.: American Oriental Society, 1974).

37. See Snellgrove, *Indo-Tibetan Buddhism*, vol. 2, p. 290.

38. There are two English translations of this text: K. Dowman, *Masters of Mahāmudrā* (Albany: State University of New York Press, 1985), and J. B. Robinson, *Buddha's Lions* (Berkeley: Dharma Publishing, 1979).

39. See Dowman, *Masters of Mahāmudrā*, pp. 216–217.

40. Ibid., p. 216.

41. Ibid.

42. Ibid., pp. 267ff.

43. Ibid., p. 272.

44. Ibid., pp. 229ff.

45. Ibid., pp. 372ff.

46. Available in two English translations: K. Dowman, *Sky Dancer* (London: Routledge & Kegan Paul, 1984), and T. Tulku, *Mother of Knowledge* (Berkeley: Dharma Publishing, 1983).

47. Dowman, *Sky Dancer*, p. 40.

48. Ibid., p. 44.

49. Ibid., p. 78.

50. Ibid., p. 86.

51. Ibid., p. 135.

52. Ibid., p. 118.
53. See T. Allione, *Woman of Wisdom* (London: Arkana, 1986), pp. 141–204.
54. Ibid., p. 168.
55. Snellgrove, *Indo-Tibetan Buddhism*, vol. 2, pp. 468–469.
56. Dowman, *Divine Madman*, pp. 46–47.
57. See H. V. Guenther, *The Life and Teaching of Naropa* (Boston: Shambhala Publications, 1986).
58. Ibid., pp. 76ff.
59. Ibid., p. 79.
60. See Nālandā Translation Committee, *Life of Marpa the Translator* (Boston: Shambhala Publications, 1986).
61. See L. P. Lhalungpa, *The Life of Milarepa* (Boston: Shambhala Publications, 1984) and G. C. C. Chang, *The Hundred Thousand Songs of Milarepa*, 2 vols. (Boston: Shambhala Publications, 1989).
62. See Chang, vol. 1, p. 20.
63. Ibid., vol. 2, p. 270ff.
64. Ibid., vol. 1, p. 177ff.
65. Ibid., p. 120.
66. Ibid., vol. 2, pp. 359–60.
67. Ibid., vol. 1, p. 146.
68. Albeit with a spiritual purpose, *The Divine Madman*, translated by Dowman, is one of the great ribald classics of world literature. What follows here is a mere sample of the racy tales of sacred sex that occur on nearly every page. The book is essential reading.
69. Dowman, *Divine Madman*, p. 42.
70. Ibid., p. 45.
71. Ibid., p. 156.
72. Ibid., p. 103.
73. Ibid., p. 96.
74. Ibid., pp. 75ff.
75. Ibid., pp. 90ff.
76. Ibid., p. 64.
77. Ibid., p. 158.
78. Ibid., p. 140.
79. See M. Aris, *Hidden Treasures and Secret Lives* (Delhi: Motilal Banarsidass, 1988); K. Dhondup, *Songs of the Sixth Dalai Lama* (Dharamsala: Library of Tibetan Works and Archives, 1981); G. W. Houston, *Wings of the White Crane* (Delhi: Motilal Banarsidass, 1982); D. Martin, "Some More Songs of the Sixth Dalai Lama," *Tibet Society Bulletin*, vol. 16 (1985): 15–18; M. Tatz, "Songs of the Sixth Dalai Lama," *The*

Tibet Journal, vol. 6 (1981): 32–36; and C. van Tuyl, "Love Songs of the Sixth Dalai Lama," *Tibet Society Newsletter,* no. 11 (1968): 4–7. For an annotated critical edition of the love songs, see P. K. Sorensen, "Tibetan Love Lyrics," *Indo-Iranian Journal,* no. 31 (1988): 253–298.

80. However, there was a strange prophecy regarding the Twelfth Dalai Lama. He was told, "If you do not practice Tantric sex you will die young." He did not practice it and died in his twenties. K. Sangpo, "Life and Times of the Eighth to Twelfth Dalai Lamas," *Tibet Journal,* vol. 7 (1982): 47–57.

81. Aris, *Hidden Treasures,* p. 123.

82. All translations of the poems in this section are my interpretations.

83. Dhondup, *Songs of the Sixth Dalai Lama,* p. 39.

84. E. Kawaguchi, *Three Years in Tibet* (Kathmandu: Ratna Pustak Bhandar, 1979), pp. 150ff.

85. The material presented here is gathered from Tachikawa-Ryū texts such as *Yoshinshū, Sangai Isshin-ki,* and *Hōkyōshū Sangen Menjū,* and the following modern studies: G. Mizuhara, *Jakyō Tachikawa Ryū* (Kyoto: Toyama Shobō, 1968); S. Moriyama, *Tachikawa Jakyō to sono Shakaitekina Haikei no Kenkyū* (Tokyo: Shikano-en, 1965); R. Sasama, *Sei no Shūkyō* (Tokyo: Daiichi Shobō, 1988); and T. Utagawa, *Shingon Tachikawa Ryū no Hihō* (Tokyo: Tokuma Books, 1981).

86. Even Snellgrove bowdlerized some sections of the *Hevajra Tantra* in his English translation.

87. Tucci, *The Theory and Practice of the Mandala,* p. 102.

88. Here is one such spell: On the night of the full moon, bathe and dress in white. Prepare a concoction out of seven specified grains and mix it with fermented milk. Boil the mixture and then place it before the bedroom door of the object of your desire. You will be sure to gain entry both into her room and her heart. (*Taizō Daizōkyō,* vol. 20, p. 425.) The Tachikawa-Ryū recommends this sex charm: prepare a figurine of the object of your desire out of powdered rice and oil; anoint it with poppyseed paste; cast it into a fire, and recite a secret mantra 1,008 times while it burns. The girl will then be yours. A recipe for an aphrodisiac from the same school: "love paper" containing the effluence of sexual intercourse and burnt pubic hair, mixed with a little of one's own blood.

89. The *Hevajra, Guhyasamāja,* and *Caṇḍamahāroṣaṇa Tantras,* for example, all contain such passages. See also M. Shenge, "Advayasiddhi," *Journal of the Oriental Institute* (Baroda: The Oriental Institute), vol. 13, no. 1 (1963): 1–30. This Tantric text, supposedly composed by a female adept, advocates that a practitioner "feast on human flesh

smeared with excrement, snatch away others' wealth, seduce their wives, and kill all the Buddhas" (p. 29).

90. Snellgrove, *Indo-Tibetan Buddhism*, vol. 1, p. 187.
91. See van Gulik, *Sexual Life*, p. 259, and Levy, *Monks and Nuns in a Sea of Sins*, p. 43.
92. E. Sharpe, *Secrets of Kaula Cirle* (London: Rider & Co., 1936), p. 100.
93. Aris, *Hidden Treasures*, p. 30.
94. There was a relationship between Zen and the Tachikawa-Ryū. The *Sangai Isshin-ki*, a basic Tachikawa text, contains many references to Zen masters, and Monkan is said to have composed this Zen verse: "Willows are green, flowers are red; things just as they are constitute the Buddhaland. The natural coupling of male and female is an adornment of Buddhahood." K. Inoue, *Monkan Jonin* (Tokyo: Jinbun Shoin, 1937), p. 55.

CHAPTER 4. THE RED THREAD OF PASSION

1. C. Luk, *Empty Cloud* (Shaftesbury: Element Books, 1977), p. 176. However, in the same book on page 173 we find this statement: "When ignorance has been permanently wiped out . . . you will be free from restraint and will enjoy independence and comfort everywhere, even in a house of prostitution, a public bar, the womb of a cow, a mare or a mule, in paradise or hell."
2. Unless otherwise noted all translations in this section are mine. For information on Layman P'ang, see R. F. Sasaki et al., *A Man of Zen* (Tokyo: John Weatherhill, 1971).
3. H. Welch, *The Practice of Chinese Buddhism* (Cambridge: Harvard University Press, 1967), p. 117.
4. Available in English translation: Li Yu, *Jou Pu Tuan* (New York: Grove Press, 1967).
5. Welch, *The Practice of Chinese Buddhism*, p. 117.
6. See Red Pine, *The Zen Teachings of Bodhidharma* (San Francisco: North Point Press, 1989), pp. 39ff., for both the original text and the translation. One of Bodhidharma's Four Great Disciples was a woman (albeit a nun).
7. This and the following verse occur in the *Wu Teng Hui Yuan*, which can be found in the *Dainihon Zoku Zōkyō*, vol. 138.
8. Translated by J. Covell and S. Yamada, *Zen's Core: Ikkyū's Freedom* (Seoul: Hollym International, 1980), p. 213.

9. There is almost nothing on Sung-yuan in English. The following information is taken from the *Sung-yuan Yu-Lu, Dainihon Zoku Zōkyō*, vol. 121.

10. This account of Tao-chi is compiled from the *Tao-chi Yu-Lu, Dainihon Zoku Zōkyō*, vol. 121.

11. See R. H. van Gulick, *Erotic Color Prints of the Ming Period* (Tokyo: privately printed, 1951), vol. 3, pp. 50–51.

12. S. Hiro, *Zen* (Tokyo: Shufu to Seikatsu Sha, 1989), p. 148.

13. See P. Rawson, *Erotic Art of the East* (New York: G. P. Putnam's Sons, 1968), pp. 292ff., and *Oriental Erotic Art* (London: Quartet Books, 1978), p. 153.

14. See P. Kronhausen and E. Kronhausen, *The Complete Book of Erotic Art* (New York: Bell Publishing, 1978), p. 271, plates 320 and 321. In China there was a similar scandal involving the princess T'ai-p'ing. She fell madly in love with a Buddhist monk from Central Asia and bestowed upon him great wealth and privilege (Chou, p. 320).

15. H. Levy, *Oriental Sex Manners* (London: New English Library, 1971), pp. 103–104.

16. See Rawson, *Erotic Art*, pp. 292ff.

17. Ibid., p. 298, plate 207.

18. See M. Takahashi, *Sei no Kami* (Kyoto: Tankōsha, 1976), pp. 143ff.

19. This was Ōnishi Ryōkei, abbot of the Kyoto's famous Kiyomizu-dera. He died in 1983 at age 106.

20. For information on Ikkyū, see S. Arntzen, *Ikkyū and the Crazy Cloud Anthology* (Tokyo: University of Tokyo Press, 1986); J. Covell and S. Yamada, *Zen's Core: Ikkyū's Freedom* (Seoul: Hollym International, 1980); and J. H. Sanford, *Zen-Man Ikkyū* (Chico, Calif.: Scholar's Press, 1981).

21. The translations of Ikkyū's poems are based on the versions found in *Ikkyū Oshō Zenshū* (Tokyo: Koshokukan, 1894); S. Kato and S. Yanagi, *Ikkyū* (Tokyo: Kodansha, 1979); and S. Nihashi, *Ikkyū: Kyōunshū* (Tokyo: Tokuma Shobō, 1974). Translations of many of the same poems also appear in the English-language studies of Ikkyū mentioned above. C. Fowkes, *The Pillow Book* (London: Hamlyn Publishing Group, 1988), contains a number of Ikkyū's poems in translation (pp. 50ff.).

22. See Sanford, *Zen-Man Ikkyū*, p. 285.

23. Ibid., pp. 283–284.

24. R. H. Blyth, *Oriental Humor* (Tokyo: Hokuseido Press, 1959), pp. 267–268.

25. For further information on Hakuin, see S. Addiss, *The Art of Zen*

(New York: Henry Abrams, 1989), pp. 102ff.; J. Stevens, "The Lively Art of Hakuin," *The East*, vol. 21, no. 2 (1984): 56–63: K. Tanahashi, *Penetrating Laughter* (Woodstock, N.Y.: Overlook Press, 1982); and P. Yampolsky, *The Zen Master Hakuin* (New York: Columbia University Press, 1971).

26. S. Kato, *Hakuin Oshō Nempyō* (Kyoto: Dohosha, 1985), p. 283.
27. Yampolsky, *Hakuin the Zen Master*, p. 188.
28. Ibid., p. 217.
29. See Tanahashi, *Penetrating Laughter*, p. 43.
30. Quoted in S. Tsuji, "Treading the Path of Zen," *The Middle Way*, vol. 64, no. 1 (May 1985). Even in Japanese Zen, there were monks who were as rigidly puritan as any follower of the Theravada. The contemporary monk Seki Seisetsu, for example, refused to let female parishioners into his room in a cancer ward: "This room is a monastery and women are not allowed in here!"
31. *Kaian Kokugō, Hakuin Oshō Zenshū* (Tokyo: Ryuginsha, 1935), vol. 3, p. 10.
32. H. Shimizu, *Josei to Zen* (Tokyo: Kokusho Hankōkai, 1915), pp. 99ff. In Korean Zen, there is an identical tale obviously based on the story of Satsu. See. S. Mitchell, *Dropping Ashes on the Buddha* (New York: Grove Press, 1976), pp. 187ff.
33. Shimizu, *Josei to Zen*, pp. 126ff.
34. See *Hakuin to sono Jidai* (Numazu: Numazu-shi Rekishi Minzoku Shiryōkan, 1983), plate 10.
35. *Hakuin Bokuseki* (Kyoto: Bokubi Sha, 1977), plate 190.
36. See Stevens, "The Lively Art of Hakuin," p. 61, and Tanahashi, *Penetrating Laughter*, p. 36.
37. See J. Stevens, "Zen and the Common Man: The Social Dimensions of Hakuin Zenji's Art," *Bulletin of the Research Institute of Buddhist Social Welfare*, no. 5 (1983): 71.
38. For further information on Sengai, see Addiss, p. 176ff; J. Stevens, "The Joy of Enlightenment: Sengai's Zen Art," *The East*, vol. 22, no. 2 (1986); and D. T. Suzuki, *Sengai, the Zen Master* (Greenwich, Conn.: New York Graphic Society, 1971).
39. See *Sengai: The Idemitsu Museum Collection* (Tokyo: Heibonsha, 1988), plates 370 and 371.
40. S. Miyake, *Sengai Gōroku* (Tokyo: Bunkensha, 1979), p. 293.
41. S. Furuta, "Sengai: Among the Cherry Blossoms, Rivers, and Willows," *Chanoyū Quarterly*, no. 22 (1979): 51.
42. S. Furuta, *Sengai* (Tokyo: Heibonsha, 1966), p. 8.
43. Miyake, *Sengai Gōroku*, p. 292.

44. In addition to the illustration included in this book, there is another version of this theme in *Sengai: The Idemitsu Museum Collection*, plate 577.
45. Ibid., plate 884.
46. Miyake, *Sengai Gōroku*, p. 298.
47. *Sengai: The Idemitsu Museum Collection*, plates 359 to 363.
48. Miyake, *Sengai Gōroku*, p. 315.
49. Ibid., p. 133.
50. *Zenmon Itsuwa Shūsei* (Kyoto: Zen Bunka Kenkyujo, 1983), vol. 1, p. 2.
51. Ibid., p. 27.
52. Miyake, *Sengai Gōroku*, p. 547.
53. *Sengai: The Idemitsu Museum Collection*, plate 508.
54. Ibid., plates 503 and 1126.
55. Miyake, *Sengai Gōroku*, p. 293.
56. Ibid., p. 291.
57. Ibid.
58. Translated by T. Legget, *A Second Zen Reader* (Tokyo: Tuttle, 1988), p. 164.
59. Hiro, *Zen*, p. 113.
60. A peony symbolizes the vulva of a sexually aroused woman. The poem is found in the manuscript copy of Seisetsu's *Bōrōshū* preserved at Shōkoku-ji in Kyoto.
61. "The Origin of Buddhist Monk's Dance," *Spring Wind*, vol. 5, no. 3 (1985): 119ff.
62. See H. N. McFarland, *Daruma* (Tokyo: Kodansha, 1987), pp. 24 and 81ff.
63. I saw this painting at an antique shop in Tokyo.
64. T. Sugano, *Zenrin Kikō* (Tokyo: Kokusho Hankokai, 1915), p. 137.
65. For an illustration of such, see Ōta, *Sei Sūhai*, p. 27.
66. See Rawson, *Oriental Erotic Art*, p. 155. Sengai did a painting of Kanzan and Jittoku with this inscription: "One is *A* [the womb realm = vulva], one is *Un* [the diamond realm = penis]; together they create the universe." *Sengai: The Idemitsu Collection*, p. 176.
67. S. Yamauchi, *Kessō Kidan* (Tokyo: Daiyukaku, 1929), pp. 65ff.
68. Legget, *A Second Zen Reader*, p. 165; Sugano, *Zenrin Kikō*, p. 25.
69. *Zenmon Itsuwa Shūsei*, vol. 1, p. 56.
70. R. Akizuki, *Zenjin* (Tokyo: Chikuma Shobō, 1983), p. 202.
71. For further information on Ryōkan, see the following by J. Stevens: *One Robe, One Bowl* (Tokyo: John Weatherhill, 1977); "Holy Foolishness," *Great Historical Figures of Japan* (Tokyo: Japan Culture Institute,

1978), pp. 209–217; and "The Life and Poetry of Ryōkan Oshō," *The East*, vol. 15 (1979): 14–20. See also Addiss, pp. 158ff., and B. Watson, *Ryōkan: Zen Monk-Poet of Japan* (New York: Columbia University Press, 1981).

72. This exchange of poems is found in Teishin's *Hasu no Tsuyu*.
73. *Zenmon Itsuwa Shūsei*, vol. 1, p. 60.
74. Ibid., pp. 59ff.
75. See W. L. and J. B. King, "Selection from Suzuki Shōsan," *The Eastern Buddhist*, vol. 12, no. 2 (1979): 126–127. See also *The Eastern Buddhist* 23, no. 1 (1990): 127. In the kōan collection *Mumonkan* there is a case (no. 42) entitled "Buddha and the Lady." The woman was next to Buddha's throne in deep meditation, a position none of Buddha's male followers could attain. The puzzle: how can this be?
76. For further information on Tesshū, see J. Stevens, *The Sword of No-Sword* (Boston: Shambhala Publications, 1989).
77. Ibid., pp. 65–66.
78. M. Takeda, *Zenki* (Tokyo: Kokusho Hankōkai, 1915), p. 16.
79. Ibid., p. 97.
80. T. Nakahara, *Nantembō Angya Roku* (Tokyo: Hirakawa Shuppansha, 1984), pp. 25–26.
81. *Zenmon Itsuwa Shūsei*, vol. 2, pp. 199ff.
82. Takeda, *Zenki*, p. 42. Musō, incidentally, was fond of the Yen-wu's "little love song" analogy and often used it in his teachings.
83. Ibid., pp. 18ff.
84. Ibid., pp. 45ff.
85. Sugano, *Zenrin Kikō*, p. 101.
86. Takeda, *Zenki*, p. 67.
87. I heard this story during a talk by a Japanese Zen master and cannot recall the particulars.
88. Takeda, *Zenki*, p. 100.
89. D. Richie, *Zen Inklings* (Tokyo: John Weatherhill, 1982), pp. 3ff. There is a contemporary Korean monk who openly sleeps with women and animals and who paints portraits of Daruma with a brush tied to his penis. Time will tell whether or not he is the genuine article. At any rate, his painting and calligraphy are vastly inferior to that of masters such as Ikkyū, Sengai, and Tesshū. See Jung-kwang, *The Mad Monk* (Berkeley: Calif.: Lancaster-Miller Publishers, 1979).
90. The origin of this kōan is not clear. Ikkyū said of it, "If a beautiful woman where to embrace this old monk, my withered willow branch would sprout right up!"

CHAPTER 5. BUDDHIST LOVE, MARRIAGE, AND SEXUAL MORALITY

1. On Tibetan marriage customs, see R. Hicks, *Hidden Tibet* (Shaftesbury: Element Books, 1988), pp. 42ff.; E. Kawaguchi, *Three Years in Tibet* (Kathmandu: Ratna Pustak Shandar, 1979), pp. 351ff.; R. J. Tung, *A Portrait of Lost Tibet* (Ithaca, N.Y.: Snow Lion Publications, 1980), pp. 97–98; H. Harrer, *Seven Years in Tibet* (Los Angeles: J. P. Tarcher, 1981), pp. 105, 124, 153, 156; N. J. Ngapo et al., *Tibet* (New York: Gallery Books, 1981), pp. 91ff. and R. D. Taring, *Daughter of Tibet* (London: Wisdom Publications, 1986).

2. See H. Iwai, "The Buddhist Priest and the Ceremony of Attaining Womanhood during the Yuan Dynasty," *Tōyōbunkō Memoirs*, no. 7 (1935): 105–161. While this service was generally requested by the parents of the girls to ensure a fertile marriage, depraved monks in China created sham rites that were supposed to help women conceive through the intercession of a "dream Buddha." Certain monks advertised that any woman who spent the night at their temple would surely become pregnant. A woman would be locked into a seemingly empty chamber. However, unbeknownst to her, she was drugged beforehand by the monks. During the night, monks emerged from hollows within the pillars, and these "dream Buddhas" would have intercourse with her. Women apparently enjoyed being ravished by phantom Buddhas and sometimes obtained the desired results, but a suspicious magistrate wanted to investigate. He hired a prostitute and told her to smear indelible rouge on each of the "Buddhas" who appeared before her. The next morning the temple was searched, and a number of monks bearing the telltale evidence were discovered. They were seized and executed, and the temple was put to the torch. Evidently such a ruse was used several times in China. See Levy, *Monks and Nuns in a Sea of Sins*, pp. 79ff., and E. W. Parsons, *Religious Chastity* (New York: AMS Press, 1975), p. 320.

3. F. Sierksma, *Tibet's Terrifying Deities* (Tokyo: Charles E. Tuttle, 1966), p. 219. Ngapo states (p. 98) that mother and daughter on occasion shared the same husband.

4. Harrer, *Seven Years in Tibet*, p. 196.

5. The lama was Pemalinga; see Aris, *Hidden Treasures and Secret Lives*, p. 27.

6. Kawaguchi, *Three Years in Tibet*, p. 352. For a sharply contrasting

view see Ngapo, pp. 89ff. Here it states that Tibetan women in the past were forced to give birth in cowsheds or sheep pens. (The present Dalai Lama in fact was born in his family's manger.) B. Aziz, in her essay "Moving Towards a Sociology of Tibet," contends that Tibetan were, and still are, treated as second-class citizens and discriminated against from birth. J. D. Willis, ed., *Feminine Ground: Essays on Women and Tibet* (Ithaca, N.Y.: Snow Lion Publications, 1989), pp. 76ff. L. S. Dowaraja in *The Position of Women in Buddhism* (Kandy: Buddhist Publication Society, 1987), pp. 1ff., maintains that women in Buddhist Burma enjoyed a high degree of independence and equality with men (the Burmese are in fact racially akin to the Tibetans). This is confirmed by W. M. Gallichan in *Women Under Polygamy* (London: Holden and Hardingham, 1914), pp. 125ff., which paints an idyllic picture of love and marriage in Burma. He states, "The Burmese girl does not wish to become a nun . . . she loves men and wishes to bear children." However, even in Burma part of a Buddhist woman's daily devotions was the prayer "to be reborn as a man as quickly as possible." Such a plea also occurs in the Tibetan Buddhist ritual, and when challenged about this the present Dalai Lama stated that such language was the result of an unfortunate cultural bias. Further, the Dalai Lama suggested that in modern society the prayer may have to be changed to, "May I not be reborn a man"! (Tsomo, p. 43.)

7. Iwai, "The Buddhist Priest," p. 115.
8. Harrer, *Seven Years in Tibet*, p. 197.
9. Ibid., p. 105.
10. Ibid., p. 124.
11. Ibid., p. 153.
12. Ibid., p. 229.
13. Ibid., pp. 197–198.
14. Ibid., p. 217.
15. Ibid.
16. Ibid., p. 89.
17. Taring, *Daughter of Tibet*.
18. T. Clifford, *Tibetan Buddhist Medicine and Psychiatry* (York Beach, Me.: Samuel Weiser, 1984), p. 104.
19. Y. Donden, *Health Through Balance* (Ithaca, N.Y.: Snow Lion Publications, 1986), p. 150.
20. J. Kunzang, *Tibetan Medicine* (Berkeley: University of California Press, 1976), p. 54.
21. Ibid., p. 285.
22. Ibid., p. 195.

23. Ibid., pp. 218–219.
24. Kawaguchi, *Three Years in Tibet*, p. 531; Sierksma, *Tibet's Terrifying Deities*, pp. 14–15. In China also it seems that Buddhist monks were once granted an annual three-day dispensation from their vows of celibacy by a sypathetic empress (Parsons, *Religious Chastity*, p. 320).
25. Sierksma, *Tibet's Terrifying Deities*, p. 169. Another Tibetan saying was, "Provide clever sons with fields and wives; send dull sons to the monastery" (S. B. Ortner, *High Religion* [Princeton: Princeton University Press, 1989], p. 183).
26. J. Blofeld, *The Wheel of Life* (Boston: Shambhala Publications, 1988), p. 85.
27. Woodward and Hare, *Gradual Sayings*, vol. 2, pp. 69–70. See also vol. 3, p. 212, where the wife tells her husband that she will not remarry if he dies; thus reassured, he survives and they continue with their happy union. Milarepa's foremost male disciple was Gambopa. He was happily married but plague claimed the lives of his two children, and then his faithful wife fell fatally ill. She clung to life, though, and refused to die peacefully. When Gambopa asked her what she was so attached to, his wife replied, "you!" Gambopa promised her that after her death he would devote himself to the Dharma and not remarry. She took his hand, gazed into his face, and died in peace. Gambopa later constructed a stupa in memory of his loving wife. Chang, vol. 1, p. 464.
28. Jātaka 267.
29. Jātaka 194.
30. "The Story of Kuddhabodhi," *The Marvelous Companion: Life Stories of the Buddha* (Berkeley, Calif.: Dharma Publishing, 1983), pp. 187.
31. Jātaka 504.
32. Jātaka 531. There are also two versions of this story in Jones, *The Mahāvastu*, vol. 3, pp. 1ff.
33. Frye, *Sūtra of the Wise and the Foolish*, pp. 73–74.
34. See, for example, the various tales in Jones, *The Mahāvastu*, vol. 2.
35. H. S. Levy, *Korean Sex Jokes in Traditional Times* (Washington D.C.: Warm-Soft Village Press, 1972), pp. 182ff.
36. Jātaka 108.
37. See G.S.D. Misra, *Development of Buddhist Ethics* (New Delhi: Munshiram Manoharlal, 1984), pp. 89ff., and H. Saddhatissa, *Buddhist Ethics* (New York: George Braziller, 1970), pp. 71ff.
38. Horner, *Middle Length Sayings*, vol. 1, p. 344. Even Tantric followers such as Drukpa Kunley had certain taboos. His were not to make love to a married woman, a girl under ten years of age, a menstruating

woman, or a woman under a strict vow of celibacy (Dowman, *Divine Madman*, p. 138).
39. Jātaka 276.
40. In Frye, *Sūtra of the Wise and the Foolish*, p. 186, a Buddhist named Aṅgulimāla has intercourse with a lioness.
41. See for example, Burlingame, *Buddhist Legends*, vol. 2, "The Hell Pot," pp. 106ff., and "The Man Who Loved Women," p. 193; and Jones, *The Mahāvastu*, vol. 1, "The Torments of Hell," pp. 6ff.
42. At one feast Buddha attended, the groom completely lost his head at the enticing sight of his bride and he wanted to have all the guests dismissed so he could take her right to bed. Buddha suddenly appeared before him and counseled: "Do not let passion get out of control; otherwise it will destroy you." The groom cooled off, and he and his bride converted to Buddhism. (Burlingame, *Buddhist Legends*, vol. 3, pp. 73ff.)
43. Tung, *A Portrait of Lost Tibet*, p. 97.
44. Kajiyama, "Woman in Buddhism," pp. 61–62.
45. Jones, *Tales and Teachings of the Buddha*, pp. 77–78.
46. Ibid., p. 133.
47. Jātaka 200.
48. Rhys Davids and Rhys Davids, *Dialogues of the Buddha*, vol. 3, pp. 181–182.
49. Woodward and Hare, *Gradual Sayings*, vol. 3, pp. 29–30.
50. Ibid., vol. 4, p. 44.
51. Jātaka 234.
52. Jātaka 276.
53. See Y. Dhonden, "Embryology in Tibetan Medicine," *Tibetan Medicine*, Series 1 (1980), Library of Tibetan Works and Archives, pp. 43–48, and L. Rinbochay and J. Hopkins, *Death, Intermediate State, and Rebirth in Tibetan Buddhism* (Ithaca, N.Y.: Snow Lion Publications, 1979), pp. 61ff.
54. See, for example, R. K. Unger, *Female and Male* (New York: Harper and Row, 1979), pp. 107ff.
55. There is mention of a most peculiar "longing of a pregnant woman." When a certain queen became with child, she begged the king to assemble an army at sunset, in full array, clad in armor, standing on auspicious ground and then to let her drink the water in which their swords were washed"! (Rhys Davids and Oldenberg, *Vinaya Texts*, vol. 2, p. 295).
56. Tibetan Buddhists supposedly developed both temporary and permanent contraceptives. (According to folklore, a Tibetan monk is sup-

posedly responsible for the invention of the "French tickler"!) However, a lama-doctor has stated that such contraceptives should only be given to women who have had seven or eight children (Dhonden, "Embryology," pp. 178–179).

57. Ibid.
58. Sodomy occurred among Buddhist monks right from Buddha's time. See Rhys Davids and Oldenberg, *Vinaya Texts*, vol. 1, p. 204.
59. *Kodansha Encyclopedia of Japan* (Tokyo: Kodansha, 1983), p. 218.
60. Sierksma, *Tibet's Terrifying Deities*, p. 223, and Harrer, *Seven Years in Tibet*, p. 217.
61. I have heard this complaint from several reliable (but necessarily unnamed) sources.
62. This is from Jiun's *Hito to naru michi*. See K. Juge, *Jiun Sonja* (Tokyo: Kodansha, 1942), pp. 366–368.
63. Jones, *The Mahāvastu*, p. 85.

Glossary

A. Mother of all sounds. The first syllable in the Tantric alphabet, *a* is regarded as the ultimate form and source of the cosmos.

AIZEN MYŌ-Ō. Tantric deity personifying all-consuming love.

ĀNANDA. Buddha's chief attendant. Ānanda knew more about the Buddha's personal habits than anyone else, and after the Master's death he was called upon to recite all that Buddha had told him. This recitation is supposed to have served as the basis of the Buddhist canon.

ANNUTTARAYOGA. The supreme method of liberation, a term employed in Vajrayāna Buddhism to represent ultimate teachings.

ARHAT. One who has attained liberation within the framework of Hīnayāna Buddhism, i.e., one who is free from all craving and is no longer subject to rebirth.

AVALOKITEŚVARA. The Bodhisattva of Compassion, usually represented in the Far East as a lovely woman.

BODHICITTA. (1) A mind set on being awakened, the basis of all Buddhist practice. (2) In Tantric Buddhism, a symbol for semen.

BODHIDHARMA. The legendary First Patriarch of Zen (Ch'an) Buddhism. Born in India, Bodhidharma brought Zen teachings to China, where he secluded himself in a cave and spent nine years in ceaseless meditation contemplating the Absolute. Bodhidharma's teaching is often summarized as follows: "Enlightenment is not found in books or in the performance of empty rites; Zen is none other than your own mind, so look within and wake up!"

BODHISATTVA. An enlightened being who works for the liberation of all, remaining in the world of samsāra rather than seeking individual release. This is the ideal of Mahāyāna Buddhism.

BUDDHA. (1) Gotama, the Indian prince who attained supreme and perfect enlightenment around 560 B.C.E. (2) An enlightened being who sees things exactly as they are in the clear light of transcendental wisdom. (3) Ultimate truth, absolute reality, perfect awakening.

BUDDHA-MIND. The innate potential for awakening possessed by all sentient beings.

BUDDHA-NATURE. The universe as a manifestation of Buddha-mind.

BUDDHISM. The multifaceted spiritual and cultural dimensions of enlightenment described, for convenience, as the teachings of Buddha. Buddhism is not an abstract doctrinal system; it does not exist independently of the present world. Buddhism, as a way of liberation, is not to be identified with any particular culture or region.

CARYA-YOGA. The practical application of Tantric teachings.

ḌĀKINĪ. Female Tantric deities who instruct and sometimes serve as sexual and spiritual consorts to male Tantric practitioners.

DEVAS. Celestial beings.

DHARMA. The Law of Buddhism, i.e., the truth of Buddhist teachings.

FUDŌ MYŌ-Ō. A Tantric deity who subdues all the enemies of the Dharma, symbolizes intense practice and unwavering devotion.

FUGEN. *See* Samantabhadra.

GASSHO. Hands joined together in a gesture of attitude and prayer.

GHEE. An Indian dish made from boiled milk.

GOTAMA. The princely name of the historical Buddha.

HERUKA. Fierce Tantric deity who emanates tremendous energy.

HĪNAYĀNA. The "Lesser Vehicle"; the more conservative tradition of Buddhism, which stresses individual effort and the necessary of monastic renunciation in order to attain liberation.

HŌJU. A fabulous jewel that grants every wish, a symbol of the treasures contained in the Buddhist teaching.

KANNON. The Japanese name for Avalokiteśvara, the Bodhisattva of Compassion.

KARMA. Cause and effect; relationships formed with people and events. In Buddhism, karma is not synonymous with fate; rather, it is a creative process that unfolds in response to both inner and outer factors.

KŌAN. An intractable puzzle given to Zen trainees to ponder during meditation; the quality of the response indicates the trainee's level of understanding.

KRIYA-YOGA. Basic Tantra, emphasizing establishment of the proper attitude for practice.

LAMA. A master teacher of Tibetan Buddhism; a lama may be either monastic or a lay practitioner.

LINGAM. The male sex organ.

MAHĀMUDRĀ. The great seal of enlightenment, a symbol of supreme liberation and enlightened consciousness in the Vajrayāna.

MAHĀYĀNA. The "Great Vehicle," the more liberal tradition of Buddhism, which emphasizes the liberation of all beings, not just a select few, and the necessity of the appropriate adjustment of Buddhist teachings to fit particular circumstances.

MANDALA. A cosmic diagram of Buddhist principles, used as an aid in the practice of visualization and meditation.

MAÑJUŚRĪ. The Bodhisattva who stands for wisdom, knowledge, and teaching.

MĀRA. The Buddhist Satan, enemy of the Dharma.

NIRVĀṆA. (1) The enlightenment attained by the historical Buddha; the extinction of all desire, distress, and illusion. (2) Supreme wisdom characterized by non-destruction, bliss, omniscience, and purity.

OM MAṆI PADME HŪM: "The jewel within the lotus all hail!" A chant used universally in Tibetan Buddhism, both as a magic spell and as a symbol of the Tantric union of male and female polarities.

ORDER OF CELIBATES. Followers of Buddhism who take strict vows of celibacy and live as monastic renunciates.

PĀYĀSA. A delectable rice pudding, said to be the dish Gotama ate prior to his awakening as the Buddha.

PRAJÑA. Wisdom; the deep insight obtained through Buddhist practice.

PRAJÑĀPARAMITĀ. The perfection of wisdom, often represented in female form in Buddhist iconography.

PURE LAND. The abode of Amitābha, the Buddha of Light, who vows to save all those who entrust themselves to his mercy. Pure Land Buddhists recite the name of Amitābha as their main practice.

SAMĀDHI. Deep contemplation, a state in which the mind is totally focused.

SAMANTABHADRA. The Bodhisattva who represents the actual application of Buddhist teachings.

SAMSĀRA. The world of pain, impermanence, and delusion, contrasted with the bliss of nirvāṇa.

SATORI. Zen enlightenment, in the sense of perception of one's innate Buddha-nature.

SHUNGA. "Pictures of spring," Japanese paintings and prints depicting lovemaking in graphic detail.

SŪTRAS. Recorded discourses attributed to Buddha; Buddhist texts in general.

TANTRA. Advanced esoteric teachings making full use of the psychophysical structure of a human being, especially the sexual dimension. Both Hinduism and Buddhism have well-established Tantric traditions.

UN. The sound of fulfillment, the last letter in the Tantric alphabet; combined with the syllable *a*, it symbolizes completion and perfection.

UPĀYA. Skillful means, the various devices a Bodhisattva can employ in order to help sentient beings attain liberation.

VAJRA. Diamond; symbol of the male sex organ.

VAJRAYĀNA. The "Diamond Vehicle," which incorporates the elements of Tantra within a Buddhist framework.

YAB-YUM. The union of mother and father; Buddhist images depicting male and female deities in sexual embrace.

YIDAM. One's personal Tantric deity, a guide to enlightenment.

YOGA. "Union," eliminating barriers between the realm of delusion and the realm of enlightenment.

YOGINI CHAKRA. A special method of making love to a number of women simultaneously, useful for kings with large harems.

YONI. The female sex organ.

ZAZEN. Formal meditation in a sitting position.

ZENDŌ. Meditation hall.

Bibliography

Addiss, S. *The Art of Zen.* New York: Henry Abrams, 1989.

Agrawal, P. K. *Mithuna.* New Delhi: Munshiram Manoharal, 1983.

Akizuki, R. *Zenjin.* Tokyo: Chikuma Shobō, 1983.

Allione, T. *Women of Wisdom.* London: Arkana, 1986.

Aris, M. *Hidden Treasures and Secret Lives.* Delhi: Motilal Banarsidass, 1988.

Arntzen, S. *Ikkyū and the Crazy Cloud Anthology.* Tokyo: University of Tokyo Press, 1986.

Aryasūra. *The Marvelous Companion.* Berkeley: Dharma Publishing, 1983.

Auboyer, J. et al. *Buddha: A Pictorial History of His Life and Legacy.* New Delhi: Roli Books International, 1983.

Bach, H. *Indian Love Paintings.* New Delhi: Lustre Press, 1985.

Bancroft, A. "Women in Buddhism." In *Women in the World's Religions.* New York: Paragon House, 1987.

Barnes, N. "Buddhism." In *Women in World Religions.* Albany: State University of New York Press, 1987.

Barrett, W. E. *Lady of the Lotus: The Untold Love Story of The Buddha and His Wife.* Los Angeles: J. P. Tarcher, 1975.

Bays, G. *The Voice of the Buddha: Lalitavistara Sutra.* Berkeley: Dharma Publishing, 1983.

Beal, S. *Fo-Sho-Hing-Tsan-King: A Life of Buddha.* Delhi: Motilal Banarsidass, 1968.

———. *The Romantic Legend of Śākya Buddha.* Delhi: Motilal Banarsidass, 1985.

Bernbaum, E. *The Way to Shambhala.* New York: Doubleday, 1980.

Bhattacharyya, N. N. *History of the Tantric Religion.* New Delhi: Manohar, 1987.

Blofeld, J. *The Wheel of Life.* Boston: Shambhala Publications, 1988.

Bunnag, J. *Buddhist Mong, Buddhist Layman.* Cambridge: Cambridge University Press, 1973.

Burlingame, E. W. *Buddhist Legends.* 3 vols. London: Pali Text Society, 1969.

Burton, R. *The Illustrated Kama Sutra.* Middlesex, England: Hamlyn, 1987.

Campbell, J. *The Masks of God: Oriental Mythology*. London: Penguin Books, 1973.

Chang, G. C. C. *The Hundred Thousand Songs of Milarepa*. 2 vols. Boston: Shambhala Publications, 1985, 1989.

———. "The True Lion's Roar of Queen Śrīmālā." In *Treasury of Mahāyāna Sutras*. University Park: Pennsylvania State University, 1983.

Ch'en, K. *Buddhism in China*. Princeton, N.J.: Princeton University Press, 1964.

Chou, I. "Tantricism in China," *Harvard Journal of Asiatic Studies* 8 (1945).

Cleary, T. *The Flower Ornament Scripture*. 3 vols. Boston: Shambhala Publications, 1984–1987.

Clifford, T. *Tibetan Buddhist Medicine and Psychiatry*. York Beach, Me.: Samuel Weiser, 1984.

Conze, E. *Buddhist Meditation*. New York: Harper and Row, 1956.

Coomaraswamy, A. *Buddha and the Gospel of Buddhism*. Secaucus, N.J.: Citadel Press, 1988.

Covell, J., and Yamada S. *Zen's Core: Ikkyū's Freedom*. Seoul: Hollym International, 1980.

Cowell, E. B. *Jātaka or Stories of the Buddha's Former Births*. 3 vols. London: Pali Text Society, 1981.

Dasgupta, S. B. *An Introduction to Tantric Buddhism*. Calcutta: University of Calcutta, 1974.

Dhondup, K. *Songs of the Sixth Dalai Lama*. Dharamsala: Library of Tibetan Works and Archives, 1981.

Donden, Y. *Health Through Balance*. Ithaca, N.Y.: Snow Lion Publications, 1986.

———. "Embryology in Tibetan Medicine." In *Tibetan Medicine*, series 1. Dharamsala: Library of Tibetan Works and Archives, 1980.

Douglas, N., and Singer, P. *The Pillow Book*. New York: Destiny Books, 1984.

———. *Sexual Secrets*. New York: Destiny Books, 1986.

Dowaraja, L. S. *The Position of Women in Buddhism*. Kandy: Buddhist Publication Society, 1987.

Dowman, K. *The Divine Madman*. Clearlake, Calif.: Dawn Horse Press, 1980.

———. *Masters of Mahāmudra*. Albany: State University of New York Press, 1985.

———. *Sky Dancer*. London: Routledge and Kegan Paul, 1984.

Fontein, J. *The Pilgrimage of Sudhana*. The Hague: Mounton and Co., 1967.

Foucher, A. *The Life of Buddha*. Wesport, Conn.: Greenwood Press, 1963.

Fowkes, C. C. *The Pillow Book*. London: Hamlyn Publishing Group, 1988.

Friedman, L. *Meetings with Remarkable Women.* Boston: Shambhala Publications, 1987.

Frye, S. *Sūtra of the Wise and the Foolish.* Dharamsala: Library of Tibetan Works and Archives, 1981.

Furuta, S. *Sengai.* Tokyo: Heibonsha, 1966.

———. "Sengai: Among the Cherry Blossoms, Rivers, and Willows." *Chanoyu Quarterly*, no. 22 (1979).

Gallichan, W. M. *Women under Polygamy.* London: Holden and Hardingham, 1914.

George, C. S. *The Candamaharosana Tantra.* New Haven, Conn.: American Oriental Society, 1974.

Goddard, D. *A Buddhist Bible.* Boston: Beacon Press, 1966.

Gombrich, R. and G. Obeyesekere. *Buddhism Transformed.* Princeton, N.J.: Princeton University Press, 1988.

Guenther, H. V. *The Life and Teaching of Naropa.* Boston: Shambhala Publications, 1986.

———. *The Royal Song of Saraha.* Seattle: University of Washington Press, 1969.

———. *The Tantric View of Life.* Boulder: Shambhala Publications, 1976.

Gyatso, J. "The Literary Transmission of the Tradition of Thang-stong rGyal-po." Ph.D. thesis, University of California, Berkeley, 1981.

Hakeda, Y. S. *Kūkai: Major Works.* New York: Columbia University Press, 1972.

Harrer, H. *Seven Years in Tibet.* Los Angeles: J. P. Tarcher, 1981.

Hecker, H. "Khemā of Great Wisdom." In *Buddhist Women at the Time of the Buddha.* Kandy: Buddhist Publication Society, 1985.

———. *Mahā Kassapa.* Kandy: Buddhist Publication Society, 1988.

Herbert, P. *The Life of the Buddha.* London: British Museum, 1990.

Hicks, R. *Hidden Tibet.* Shaftesbury: Element Books, 1988.

Hirakawa, A. *Monastic Discipline for the Buddhist Nuns.* Patna: Kashi Prasad Jayaswal Research Institute, 1982.

Hiro, S. *Zen.* Tokyo: Shufu to Seikatsu Sha, 1989.

Horner, I. B. *Book of The Discipline.* 6 vols. London: Pali Text Society, 1982.

———. *The Collection of Middle Length Sayings.* 3 vols. London: Pali Text Society, 1979.

———. *Women in Primitive Buddhism.* Delhi: Motilal Banarsidass, 1975.

Houston, G. W. *Wings of the White Crane.* Delhi: Motilal Banarsidass, 1982.

Huntington, S., and J. Huntington. *The Art of Ancient India.* Tokyo: John Weatherhill, 1987.

Ikkyū. *Ikkyū Oshō Zenshū.* Tokyo: Koshokan, 1984.

Inoue, K. *Monkan Jonin.* Tokyo: *Jinbun Shoin,* 1937.

Inwood, K. *Bhikku, Disciple of the Buddha.* Bangkok: Thai Watona Panich, 1981.

Iwai, H. "The Buddhist Priest and the Ceremony of Attaining Woman-hood during the Yuan Dynasty." *Tōyōbunkō Memoirs,* no. 7 (1935).

Iwamoto, Y. *Bukkyō to Josei.* Tokyo: Daisan-Bunmei, 1986.

Johnston, E. H. *The Buddhacarita or Acts of the Buddha.* Delhi: Motilal Banarsidass, 1984.

———. *The Saundarananda of Aśvoghoṣa.* Delhi: Motilal Banarsidass, 1988.

Jones, J. *The Tales and Teachings of the Buddha.* London: George Allen and Unwin, 1979.

Jones, J. J. *The Mahāvastu.* 3 vols. London: Pali Text Society, 1973.

Jootla, S. E. *Inspiration from Enlightened Nuns.* Kandy: Buddhist Publication Society, 1988.

Juge, K. *Jiun Sonja.* Tokyo: Kodansha, 1942.

Jung-Kwang. *The Mad Monk.* Berkeley: Lancaster-Miller Publishers, 1979.

Kajiyama, Y. "Women in Buddhism." *Eastern Buddhist* 15, no. 2 (1982).

Kalupahana, D. J., and I. Kalupahana. *The Way of Siddhartha: A Life of the Buddha.* Boulder: Shambhala Publications, 1983.

Katō, S. and S. Yanagi. *Ikkyū.* Tokyo: Kodansha, 1979.

Kawaguchi, E. *Three Years in Tibet.* Kathmandu: Ratna Pustak Bhandar, 1979.

Khantipalo. *Bag of Bones.* Kandy: Buddhist Publication Society, 1980.

———. *The Path of Freedom: Vimittimagga.* Kandy: Buddhist Publication Society, 1977.

King, W. L., and J. B. King. "Selections from Suzuki Shōsan." *The Eastern Buddhist* 12, no. 2 (1979).

Krom, N. J. *The Life of Buddha on the Stupa of Barabudar.* New Delhi: Bhartiya Publishing House, 1974.

Kronhausen, P., and E. Kronhausen. *The Complete Book of Erotic Art.* New York: Bell Publishing, 1978.

Ku, K. *The Mahāyāna View of Woman: A Doctrinal Study.* Madison: University of Wisconsin, 1984.

Kunzang, J. *Tibetan Medicine.* Berkeley: University of California Press, 1976.

Lamotte, E. *The Teaching of Vimalakīrti.* London: Pali Text Society, 1976.

Legget, T. *A Second Zen Reader.* Tokyo: Tuttle, 1988.

Lester, R. *Theravada Buddhism in Southeast Asia.* Ann Arbor: University of Michigan Press, 1973.

Levy, H. S. *Chinese Sex Jokes in Traditional Times.* Washington, D.C.: Warm-Soft Press, 1973.

177

―――. *Japanese Sex Jokes in Traditional Times.* Washington, D.C.: Warm-Soft Press, 1973.

―――. *Korean Sex Jokes in Traditional Times.* Washington, D.C.: Warm-Soft Press, 1972.

―――. *Monks and Nuns in a Sea of Sins.* Taipei: Chinese Association for Folklore, 1975.

―――. *Oriental Sex Manners.* London: New English Library, 1971.

Lhalungpa, L. P. *The Life of Milarepa.* Boston: Shambhala Publications, 1984.

Lillie, A. *The Life of Buddha.* Delhi: Seema Publications, 1974.

Li Yu. *Jou Pu Tan.* New York: Grove Press, 1967.

Luk, C. *Empty Cloud.* Shaftesbury: Element Books, 1977.

―――. *The Vimalakīrti Nirdeśa Sūtra.* Boston: Shambhala Publications, 1990.

McFarland, H. N. *Daruma.* Tokyo: Kōdansha, 1987.

Mackenzie, V. *Reincarnation: The Boy Lama.* London: Bloomsbury, 1988.

Martin, D. "Some More Songs of the Sixth Dalai Lama." *Tibet Society Bulletin* 16 (1985).

Michael, G., et al. *In the Image of Man.* London: Weidenfeld and Nicolson, 1982.

Misra, G. S. P. *Development of Buddhist Ethics.* New Delhi: Munishiram Monoharlal, 1984.

Mitchell, S. *Dropping Ashes on the Buddha.* New York: Grove Press, 1976.

Miyake, S. *Sengai Gōroku.* Tokyo: Bunkensha, 1979.

Mizuhara, G. *Jakyō Tachikawa Ryu.* Kyoto: Toyama Shobō, 1968.

Morita, S. *Hakuin Bokuseki.* Kyoto: Bokubisha, 1977.

Moriyama, S. *Tachikawa Jakyō to sono Shakaitekina Haikei no Kenkyū.* Tokyo: Shikano-en, 1965.

Nakahara, T. *Nantembō Angya Roku.* Tokyo: Hirakawa Shuppansha, 1984.

Nakamura, H. *Gotama Buddha.* Los Angeles and Tokyo: Buddhist Books International, 1977.

Nālandā Translation Committee. *Life of Marpa the Translator.* Boston: Shambhala Publications, 1986.

Nanamoli. *The Life of the The Buddha.* Kandy: Buddhist Publication Society, 1972.

Ngapo, N. J. et al. *Tibet.* New York: Gallery Books, 1981.

Nihashi, S. *Ikkyū: Kyōunshū.* Tokyo: Tokuma Shobō, 1974.

Obermiller, E. *Bu-ston: History of Buddhism.* Heidelberg: privately published, 1932.

Ota, S. *Sei Sūhai.* Tokyo: Reimei Shobo, 1986.

Ortner, S. B. *High Religion*. Princeton, N.J.: Princeton University Press, 1989.

Pandit. V. L. *Woman Saints of East and West*. London: Ramakrishna Vedanta Center, 1955.

Parsons, E. W. *Religious Chastity*. New York: AMS Press, 1975.

Paul, D. *Women in Buddhism*. Berkeley: Asian Humanities Press, 1979.

Poppe, N. *Twelve Deeds of Buddha*. Wiesbaden: Otto Harrassowitz, 1967.

Prasad, S. N. *Kalyāṇamalla's Anaṅgaraṅga*. New Delhi: Chaukhambha Orientalia, 1983.

Puri, B.N. *Buddhism in Central Asia*. Delhi: Motilal Banarsidass, 1987.

Rawson, P. *Erotic Art of the East*. New York: G.P. Putnam's Sons, 1968.

———. *Oriental Erotic Art*. London: Quartet Books, 1987.

Red Pine. *The Zen Teachings of Bodhidharma*. San Francisco: North Point Press, 1989.

Rexroth, K., ed. *The Buddhist Writings of Lafcadio Hearn*. London: Wildwood House, 1981.

Rhys Davids, C. A. F., and F. L. Woodward. *The Book of Kindred Sayings*. 5 vols. London: Pali Text Society, 1979.

Rhys Davids, T. W., and C. A. F. Rhys Davids. *Dialogues of the Buddha*. 3 vols. London: Pali Text Society, 1977.

Rhys Davids, T. W., and H. Oldenberg. *Vinaya Texts*. 3 vols. Delhi: Motilal Banarsidass, 1968.

Richie, D. *Zen Inlings*. Tokyo: John Weatherhill, 1982.

Rinbochay, L., and J. Hopkins. *Death, Intermediate State, and Rebirth in Tibetan Buddhism*. Ithaca, N.Y.: Snow Lion Publications, 1979.

Robinson, J. B. *Buddha's Lions*. Berkeley: Dharma Publishing, 1979.

Rockwell, W. W. *The Life of Buddha*. London: Trubner's Oriental Series, 1884.

Saddhatissa, H. *Buddhist Ethics*. New York: George Braziller, 1970.

Sanford, J. H. *Zen-Man Ikkyū*. Chico, Calif.: Scholar's Press, 1981.

Sangpo, K. "Life and Times of the Eighth to Twelfth Dalai Lamas." *Tibet Journal* 7 (1982).

Sasaki, R. F., et al. *A Man of Zen*. Tokyo: John Weatherhill, 1971.

Sasama, R. *Sei no Shūkyō*. Tokyo: Dai-ichi Shobo, 1988.

Sharpe, E. *Secrets of Kaula Circle*. London: Rider and Co., 1936.

Shenge, M. "Advayasiddhi." *Journal of the Oriental Institute* 13, no. 1. Baroda: Oriental Institute, 1963.

Shimizu, H. *Josei to Zen*. Tokyo: Kokusho Hankokai, 1915.

Siegal, L. *Laughing Matters*. Chicago: University of Chicago Press, 1987.

Sierksma, F. *Tibet's Terrifying Deities*. Tokyo: Charles E. Tuttle, 1966.

Snellgrove, D. *Indo-Tibetan Buddhism*. 2 vols. Boston: Shambhala Publications, 1988.

―――. *The Image of the Buddha*. Tokyo: Kōdansha International, 1978.

Sorensen, P. K. "Tibetan Love Lyrics." *Indo-Iranian Journal*, no. 31 (1988).

Spiro, M. E. *Buddhism and Society*. New York: Harper and Row, 1963.

Stevens, J. *One Robe, One Bowl*. Tokyo: John Weatherhill, 1977.

―――. *The Sword of No-Sword: Life of the Master Warrior Tesshū*. Boston: Shambhala Publications, 1989.

Suematsu, R. *Sengai: The Idemitsu Museum Collection*. Tokyo: Heibousha, 1988.

Sugano, T. *Zenrin Kikō*. Tokyo: Kokusho Hankokai, 1915.

Sunim, M. S. *Thousand Peaks*. Berkeley: Parallax Press, 1987.

Suzuki, D. T. *Essays in Zen Buddhism*, Third Series. London: Rider and Co., 1953.

―――. *Sengai, the Zen Master*. Greenwich, Conn.: New York Graphic Society, 1971.

Takahashi, M. *Sei no Kami*. Kyoto: Tankosha, 1976.

Takeda, M. *Zenki*. Tokyo: Kokusho Hankōkai, 1915.

Tanahashi, K. *Penetrating Laughter*. Woodstock, N.Y.: Overlook Press, 1982.

Taring, R. D. *Daughter of Tibet*. London: Wisdom Publications, 1986.

Tatz, M. "Songs of the Sixth Dalai Lama." *Tibet Journal* 6 (1981).

Thera, P. *The Virgin's Eye*. Kandy: Buddhist Publication Society, 1980.

Thomas, E. J. *The Life of Buddha as Legend and History*. London: Routledge and Kegan Paul, 1969.

Thurman, R. A. F. *The Holy Teaching of Vimilakirti*. University Park: Pennsylvania State University, 1976.

Tsomo, K. L. *Sakyadhītā: Daughters of the Buddha*. Ithaca, N.Y.: Snow Lion Publications, 1988.

Tsuji, S. "Treading the Path of Zen." *The Middle Way* 64, no. 1 (May 1985).

Tucci, G. *The Theory and Practice of the Mandala*. London: Rider and Co., 1961.

―――. *Rati-Līlā*. Geneva: Nagel Publishers, 1969.

Tulku, T. *Mother of Knowledge*. Berkeley: Dharma Publishing, 1983.

Tung, R. J. *A Portrait of Lost Tibet*. Ithaca, N.Y.: Snow Lion Publications, 1980.

Unger, R. K. *Female and Male*. New York: Harper and Row, 1979.

Utagawa, T. *Shingon Tachikawa Ryū no Hihō*. Tokyo: Tokuma Books, 1981.

van Gulick, R. H. *Erotic Color Prints of the Ming Period.* Tokyo: privately published, 1951.

———. *Sexual Life in Ancient China.* Leiden: E.J. Brill, 1974.

van Tuyl, C. "Love Songs of the Sixth Dalai Lama." *Tibet Society Newsletter,* no. 2 (1968).

Warren, H. C. *Buddhism in Translation.* Cambridge, Mass.: Harvard University Press, 1986.

Watson, B. *Ryōkan: Zen Monk-Poet of Japan.* New York: Columbia University Press, 1981.

Wayman, A., and H. Wayman. *The Lion's Roar of Queen Śrīmālā.* New York: Columbia University Press, 1974.

Welch, H. *The Practice of Chinese Buddhism.* Cambridge, Mass.: Harvard University Press, 1967.

Willis, J. D., ed. *Feminine Ground: Essays on Women and Tibet.* Ithaca, N.Y.: Snow Lion Publications, 1985.

Windsor, E. *The Hindu Art of Love.* New York: Panurge Press, 1932.

Woodward, F. L., and E. M. Hare. *The Book of Gradual Sayings.* 5 vols. London: Pali Text Society, 1979.

Yamauchi, S. *Kessō Kidan.* Tokyo: Daiyukaku, 1929.

Yampolsky, P. *The Platform Sutra of the Sixth Patriarch.* New York: Columbia University Press, 1967.

———. *The Zen Master Hakuin.* New York: Columbia University Press, 1971.

Zen Bunka Kenkyūjō, ed. *Zenmon Itsuwa Shusei.* 3 vols. Kyoto: Zen Bunka Kenkyūjō, 1983.

Zwalf, W. *Buddhism: Art and Faith.* London: British Museums Publications, 1985.

Index

Index